Praise for *Heaven Revealed*

Often we hear that Christians spend too much time thinking about heaven. Actually, the opposite is true. Far too many of today's believers are uninformed about heaven and fail to understand why we should be yearning for the fullness that God has for us in eternity. Paul Enns offers a corrective to our neglect of heaven in **Heaven Revealed**. *You will be greatly blessed by this book.*

Dr. R. Albert Mohler Jr., president
The Southern Baptist Theological Seminary

Paul Enns has thought carefully about heaven ever since his beloved wife, Helen, died unexpectedly a few years ago. The result is a book that is a wonderful blend of biblical insight and human longings, coupled with the personal assurance that we shall meet one another again in heaven. This is a delightful read for those who have lost loved ones, and for those of us who need an injection of biblical hope during these times of worldly struggles and distress. Paul has blessed the body of Christ by opening a window into the life beyond. Just read ⁺¹ ⁻ew pages, and you will want to read to the end.*

Dr. Erwin W. Lutzer
The Moody Chu

This book was written in the ₚₐₙ *and loss; the death of a beloved spouse. It is* ₓy *biblical conviction, theological faithfulness, and pastoral sensitivity. Those who read it will have their minds instructed, their hearts comforted, and their wills fortified as they long to see King Jesus face to face.*

Dr. Daniel Akin, president
Southeastern Baptist Theological Seminary

WHAT IS IT LIKE?
WHAT WILL WE DO?

AND 11 OTHER THINGS YOU'VE WONDERED ABOUT

HEAVEN REVEALED

PAUL ENNS

MOODY PUBLISHERS
CHICAGO

© 2011 by
PAUL ENNS

Scripture quotations are taken from the *New American Standard Bible*®, Copyright © 1960, 1962, 1963, 1968, 1971, 1972, 1973, 1975, 1977, 1995 by The Lockman Foundation. Used by permission. (www.Lockman.org)

Edited by Jim Vincent
Interior design: Smartt Guys design
Cover design: Tan Nguyen
Cover image: iStockphoto

Library of Congress Cataloging-in-Publication Data

Enns, Paul P., 1937-
    Heaven revealed : what is it like? what will we do? ... and 11 other
things you've wondered about / Paul Enns.
        p. cm.
    Includes bibliographical references.
    ISBN 978-0-8024-4982-5
    1. Heaven—Christianity. I. Title.

BT846.3.E56 2011
236'.24—dc22
                                            2010029364

We hope you enjoy this book from Moody Publishers. Our goal is to provide high-quality, thought-provoking books and products that connect truth to your real needs and challenges. For more information on other books and products written and produced from a biblical perspective, go to www.moodypublishers.com or write to:

Moody Publishers
820 N. LaSalle Boulevard
Chicago, IL 60610

1 3 5 7 9 10 8 6 4 2

Printed in the United States of America

*To the Enns, Klassen, Schroeder, and Paetkau families
of the past five hundred years, all ancestors
of Helen and myself,
for their integrity, industry, and, above all,
their God-fearing nature and devotion to Christ,
which encompassed their entire lives.*

*And to my immediate family:
Terry and Raye Jeanne, Elizabeth and Emily,
Jeremy and Kim, Jacob, Joel, and Addison.*

*And to my beloved Helen,
who preceded me to heaven
and whom I eagerly long for in reunion.*

Contents

INTRODUCTION:

My STORY

After I had parked the car, Helen and I walked to the sanctuary, holding hands as we always did when we walked together. We had been husband and wife for forty-five years, yet I still felt like a newly engaged young man, smitten with love and thrilled by holding hands with the one he loves.

Our pastor, Ken Whitten, became emotional and teary-eyed that Sunday evening as he spoke during the sermon of being with his father just before he died. Pastor Ken recalled how he told his father, "I'll meet you at the tree of life."

I leaned over to Helen and told her, "I'll meet you at the Eastern Gate." She smiled and responded in agreement.

After the service we visited with numerous people (as Helen loved to do) and finally walked to the car, hand in hand. I opened the car door for her, and soon we were on our way home.

I was unusually tired that evening and headed for bed ahead of Helen. When she came to bed I was almost asleep, so I missed our nightly ritual. Before turning out the light we would clasp hands, and Helen would say, *"Gutte nacht, mein schatz!"* ("Good night, my treasure!") I would respond, *"Gutte nacht, mein schatze!"* ("Good night, my little treasure!")

The next morning, as I was leaving the house to drive to Idlewild Baptist Church to teach an extension seminary class, Helen walked to the car with me—as she always did. She carried my mug of coffee, took a few sips (she wasn't supposed to drink coffee since it made her heart act up), and then handed me the cup. She was wearing walking shorts.

"Go inside, it's too cold," I suggested. But I knew she wouldn't go in. Whenever I drove away, she would always wave me off. I backed out of the driveway, and as I drove away she blew me some kisses and then waved to me. She was now in the street, and continued to wave until I turned the corner at the far end of the street. Our love was simple and sincere. We never got over the thrill and joy of the love we had for each other.

That morning, as I taught about the bodily resurrection of Christ, I became emotional and began to cry. I couldn't explain it. At two o'clock I finished teaching the class but stayed for another half-hour talking to the students.

I arrived home about 2:45 p.m. to find the door was locked. That was unusual, since Helen would always unlock the door when she knew I was coming home. I unlocked the door and entered the house. "Helen," I called. No answer. I called louder, "HELEN!" Still no answer. *She must be working outside,* I told myself. I put down my briefcase and walked into the kitchen.

I screamed as I saw Helen lying face down on the kitchen floor. I ran to her, turned her over, but there was no movement. "HELEN, HELEN!" I shouted. I ran to the kitchen phone and quickly dialed 911, crying and screaming at the same time.

The lady admonished me to calm down, so I could help Helen. I followed her instruction and gave Helen mouth-to-mouth resuscitation, pumping her chest as I was told to do. In a short time the ambulance arrived, and the men took over.

For over an hour they sought to revive Helen. Finally, they came to me and said, "We could take her to the hospital, but the line is flat. She's gone."

Words are incapable of describing my emotion at that moment. My beloved Helen was gone! I couldn't begin to fathom that it had actually happened. Helen gone! I couldn't fathom it. *It's not true! It can't be!*

I had never gotten over the thrill of Helen. From the moment I laid my eyes on her smiling face and happy eyes, I was captivated by her. I have told people I was on a forty-five-year honeymoon. Now she was gone.

Death is a harsh reality, one we don't like to relate to ourselves. Helen and I had recently talked, and she had mentioned that we both have longevity in our blood, and we planned what we would do when we hit our eighties. But Helen was only sixty-five, and now she was gone from me. But death encompasses everyone. As someone has said, "Death is all-inclusive; it's one out of one."

THOUGHTS OF HEAVEN

That singular event has changed my life and my thinking. My thoughts are constantly focused on heaven. I'm absorbed with the thought of heaven. The thought of reunion with my beloved Helen!

But that raises many questions. What is heaven like? Will we know one another? What will be our relationships if we do know each other? Will we have physical bodies? How will we relate to each other—will we eat together and fellowship together? Will we all live in the New Jerusalem? Will there be a new world that we relate to? What will we do in heaven? Will we retain our ethnic identities? On and on, so many questions.

Searching books that described end-time events produced some astonishing results. I found that well-known biblicists who wrote prolifically on the rapture, the tribulation, the second coming, and the millennium had little to say about heaven.

Many had concluded that the Old Testament prophecies deal with the millennium but have nothing to say about heaven. Yet when I investigated some of the passages, I saw words like "forever," "for all time," and "shall never end." Were those words to be restricted to one thousand years? Or does "forever" mean "forever"? The key question then becomes, "Is there a continuity between the millennium and the eternal state?" If so, the millennial passages then provide significant insight into what we refer to as "heaven."

Helen's homegoing has hit me hard. It has radically changed my thinking. I am consumed with the thought of heaven. Not that we had a complicated life before; we didn't. We watched almost no television and never got immersed in technology issues—friends were always trying to bring me into the twentieth century! We rarely went to movies; in our forty-five years of marriage we probably didn't go to more than five or six. I have been absorbed in the ministry: teaching seminary classes, performing pastoral ministry, and writing. I was able to be engrossed in ministry because Helen did everything at home—inside the house and outside. She set me free to do the ministry. I didn't have a clue about things in the house. I told the folks at the church that I had never run a dishwasher, a clothes washer, a dryer; I'd never ironed a piece of clothing in my life; I'd never baked anything in the oven. (When I tried to bake something recently, the plastic lid melted and was absorbed into the food.) Helen did all those things at home— and in that she truly partnered with me in the ministry. What a fabulous wife she was!

But Helen was not only my wife; she was also my best friend. I'd usually shut down my studies at 5:30 p.m., and we'd sit in the living room or sunroom and visit for two hours—yes, two hours. We would plan our next trip to Austria or reminisce about past trips and events. We had lots to talk about. We were best friends. With my wife, my best friend gone, my mind is focused on heaven.

When Pastor Whitten asked me to preach one Wednesday, I immediately told him, "I know what I'm going to preach on."

"You do?" he asked.

"Yes," I said. "Heaven."

And I did. Before I preached, I asked the congregation a question. "Who has a loved one, a wife, a husband, a child, a parent, or a friend who is in heaven?"

Every hand went up. There was no one who didn't have a loved one who had gone ahead into heaven. And so I preached on heaven. It was an outpouring of a broken heart, a grieving heart. I had previously told the people that I had been on a forty-five year honeymoon. They knew I had never gotten over the thrill of Helen.

COMFORT FROM THE SCRIPTURES

So I preached on heaven. The questions foremost in my mind—and in the minds of many people—are whether we will know one another in heaven and what our relationship will be. As I preached, I let the Scriptures speak for themselves, but as I pored over the applicable Scriptures, my heart was greatly comforted.

Yes, we will know one another! Yes, we will have a glorious reunion! The Scriptures are not unclear on this vital issue.

As I shared my biblical study with the people, I sensed a strong, positive response. The people also were comforted and encouraged. Afterward, several came to me and said, "I have finally been able to put closure on it." The response to the sermon was phenomenal—because of the subject.

People are interested in heaven. Everyone has someone in heaven, and they have questions. Valid questions. And thankfully, the Scriptures have a lot to say about heaven. Unfortunately, some have dismissed a knowledge of heaven by saying, "We don't know very much about the new heaven and the new earth." Wrong. The Scriptures have a lot to say about where we as redeemed believers will spend eternity. And the words are comforting and encouraging.

That does not mean my heartsickness is fully past. I still feel numb at times. Not angry, just broken and numb. People have told me to express anger at God, but I haven't and I can't. I haven't changed my doctrinal beliefs. I still believe that our days are numbered as the Bible states, "Since his days are determined, the number of his months is with You" (Job 14:5). Even before we were born our days were appointed (see Ps. 139:16). I still believe that. God has appointed the days for Helen and the days for me. I just wish that He had appointed more days for her. I'm lonely—very lonely—without her, and no one else can fill that void.

EARTH'S SHADOW

Recently an elderly man asked me, "Will we know one another in heaven?" He was concerned as both he and his wife are on in years. I said, "I will answer your question generally and specifically. First, generally. That is heaven; this is earth. Think of the words. *Heaven. Earth.* Heaven is *always* better, in every realm, in *every dimension.* How could heaven be heaven if there was one arena in which heaven would be poorer and inferior to conditions on earth? It wouldn't be heaven! You and I cannot think of a single realm or phase of living in which life would be poorer in heaven. Health? Better! Knowledge? Excessively better! Relationships? Much better! Everything will be better in every area of life."

With that, I told him, "I will also answer you specifically. Yes, we will know one another, better and in a more intense loving relationship than we ever had on earth." What a phenomenal, encouraging thought!

Meanwhile life continues for us on this present earth. Yet we're told life for you and me is a shadow of what it will be in heaven. Hebrews 8:5 reminds us that these earthly things serve as "a copy and shadow of the heavenly things." The writer refers to the Old Testament worship system as being only a shadow of real worship as it will one day be in glory. The application, however, can extend to every realm of living on this earth.

Just as the Old Testament system is but a shadow of ultimate worship of God, its fulfillment is in Christ (Col. 2:17; cf. Heb. 10:1). But Christ is not ruling on earth today as so many prophets have promised; therefore, the reality must still be future—fulfilled on the new earth.

Creation itself groans, anticipating that glorious day when Christ will rule on the new earth forever, when even creation will be restored to pristine, unfallen condition: "For the anxious longing of the creation waits eagerly for the revealing of the sons of God" (Rom. 8:19). Creation is pictured, as with outstretched neck, longing for the day when this earth will be renovated, renewed, and restored to its God-ordained condition. And as creation groans in anticipation of Christ's eternal rule on earth, so we too, "groan within ourselves, waiting eagerly for our adoption as sons, the redemption of our body" (Rom. 8:23).

This is *the* day. There is a day coming when all of the suffering, all of the maladies of this life are destroyed, when we, in our glorified bodies, will live in heaven, on the new earth, eternally fulfilling God's ordained purpose for us. We too yearn and wait for that day. And we will live in fellowship with God and with our redeemed loved ones in a perfect environment, in a heaven of indescribable beauty and perfect environment.

In this study we will examine Scripture passages that speak of our glorious future, of heaven, of the glory of God, of our relationships with loved ones, of our environment, and of our activity in heaven.

The Bible has a great deal to say about life in heaven. And it is a glorious, wonderful hope.

FUTURE FOCUS: HEAVEN

But that future, that hope of heaven, should help us focus our lives properly on this life, having an eternal perspective. While I was a student in college, a visiting speaker in chapel exhorted us, "Don't be so heavenly minded that you're no earthly good." I never forgot that statement. I've reflected on it. The chapel speaker was *wrong*, decidedly wrong. We could transpose the statement to read correctly: "Unless you are heavenly minded, you won't be any earthly good." There are numerous passages that remind us of this biblical truth, to have our focus on heaven, not on earth (cf. Matt. 6:33; Rom. 12:2; Col. 3:1–4; Heb. 11:10, 16). It is only as we fixate our eyes—our thoughts—on our future hope in heaven that we will be strengthened and enabled to live wisely in this life.

That hope of heaven alone will be our comfort and encouragement as we wander through this life. We are pilgrims looking for another world, a better world. Nothing else on this earth can provide that incomparable comfort, that ultimate resolution to our greatest dilemma —to anticipate a glorious, unending reunion and fellowship with loved ones, never, never to end. Read on ...

What Is the MEANING
of HEAVEN?

A college professor described a recent discussion about heaven with his friend. "With the look of a man who has been invited to a dull party and cannot decline, my best friend confided that he was worried about heaven."

"'I know we're supposed to look forward to being in heaven,' the friend explained. 'But when I read the book of Revelation, it looks like all we will be doing is bowing up and down.

"'Up and down,' he repeated in a note of despair. 'Up and down for all eternity!'"[1]

People—including Christians—develop strange, unbiblical views of heaven. The notions about heaven that many people have do not come from Scripture; rather, it is their *failure* to study Scripture that has led to a lack of knowledge and understanding of the biblical meaning of heaven.

What is heaven? People use the word *heaven* to describe the grandeur of secular things, entirely unrelated to the biblical concept.

Others see heaven as a mystical place in the clouds with an unending church service. Many concepts of heaven are without scriptural warrant. The word *heaven* is used in three different ways in Scripture to describe the atmospheric heaven, the celestial heaven, and "the third heaven." Additionally, there are related words that further describe heaven: *paradise* (known also as *the intermediate heaven*), *the new heaven and the new earth*, and *the New Jerusalem*.

THE ATMOSPHERIC HEAVEN

As a young boy I liked to lie on the lawn and look up at the sky, watching the cloud formations and imagine what they were: animals, people—my imagination was limitless in speculating about what I was seeing. That is the atmospheric heaven we see.

Heaven is sometimes used to describe the troposphere—the space surrounding the earth and extending outward to a height of about six miles. This is the atmospheric heaven from which the earth receives dew (Deut. 33:13), frost (Job 38:29), rain and snow (Isa. 55:10), wind (Job 26:13), and thunder (1 Sam. 2:10). The clouds are in the atmospheric heaven (Ps. 147:8), and the birds fly in it (Gen. 1:20).

Since the dew, rain, snow, and wind come from "heaven," it is a reminder of God's gracious gift to all humanity (Matt. 5:45).

THE CELESTIAL HEAVEN

Heaven is also used to describe the celestial realm—the realm of the sun, moon, stars, and planets. This is the universe. God created the universe (Gen. 1:1; Ps. 33:6), placing these lights in the celestial heaven (Gen. 1:14). Scientists have discovered a star that is so large, if it were hollow, it could contain our entire solar system with the sun at the center and all the planets revolving around the sun. This is but one reminder of the vastness of the celestial heaven that God created.

THE THIRD HEAVEN

Heaven, as the dwelling place of God, is also called "the third heaven." This is truly "the heaven of heavens, the abode of God."[2] The apostle Paul was "caught up to the third heaven" and given a glimpse of heaven's glory, to sustain him in the time of suffering, reminding him of the magnificent glory that awaited him (2 Cor. 12:2). "Paul was granted the sight of the glory that lies ahead and was thereby fortified to enter patiently all the suffering which awaited him"[3] This is a reminder to us that amid the suffering and trials of life, a heavenly perspective is necessary. Only those who keep their eyes fixed on the glory to come will endure the trials and sufferings in the present.

Like Paul, the apostle John was caught up into heaven (Rev. 4:1ff.). As John was transported to heaven, he saw "One sitting on the throne" (Rev. 4:2). John saw the twenty-four elders, the royal attendants, and the *shekinah* of God in all the brilliance of the Majestic Glory. Truly, heaven is the dwelling place of the glory of God.

God is enthroned in heaven (v. 2) from where He governs the affairs of nations and scoffs at their inept efforts in rebellion against His authority (Ps. 2:4). God's rule in heaven is a reminder that His purpose will be accomplished; Christ will ultimately rule in triumph over the nations (Ps. 2:6–9).

Heaven is where God dwells. It is a specific place; it is not a simply a state. It is incorrect to define it as essentially a state. Heaven is a *place*. Jesus reminded His disciples to pray, "Our Father who is in heaven" (Matt. 6:9). It is the place Jesus has gone to prepare for His own and has promised to come back and bring us to live with Him in heaven (John 14:2–3). John tells us of the new heaven and the new earth and the New Jerusalem coming down out of heaven from God—which is what Jesus has gone to prepare for us (Rev. 21:1–2).

Heaven is a place of unparalleled tranquility and beauty (Rev. 21:1–22:7). It includes the new heaven and new earth (Rev. 21:1) and the holy city, the New Jerusalem (Rev. 21:2). It is the place where God will dwell with His people and have intimate fellowship with them (Rev. 21:3).

PARADISE

As I mention elsewhere in this book, Cypress Gardens was a favorite place for Helen and me to visit and relax amid the magnificent scenery. Located in central Florida, Cypress Gardens reveals the colorful creation of God. The rich, red, cascading bougainvillea bloom throughout most of the year; the spring flower festival with the brilliant poinsettias, azaleas, and many other beautiful flowers decorate the park. They are a reminder of God's magnificent creation—and a reminder of paradise.

Heaven is also called "paradise," where Paul heard "inexpressible words, which a man is not permitted to speak" (2 Cor. 12:4). These are words "often used of divine secrets which were not intended for human beings."[4]

Paradise is pictured as a garden, originally describing the parks of the Persian king.[5] It also is depicted as the garden of Eden, the creation of God (Gen. 2:8–10). In the garden of Eden, God "caused to grow every tree that is pleasing to the sight and good for food" (v. 9). A river flowed out of Eden to water the garden (v. 10). The picturesque language reveals the unparalleled beauty of the garden of Eden. The lush flora and fauna was not only God's provision for food, but also a picture of beauty. Visitors to the Butchart Gardens on Canada's Vancouver Island, the Sissinghurst Castle Garden in Kent, England, with its White Garden, Rose Garden, Cottage Garden, and Lime Walk, or other magnificent gardens in the world today can only imagine how beautiful the garden of Eden must have been. It would have surpassed any floral beauty that exists today in our fallen world.

Unquestionably, there is a continuity between the garden of Eden in Genesis and the paradise envisioned at the end of the age. In the pre-Christian era it was recognized "that the paradise of the first age reappears in that of the last. The site of reopened Paradise is almost without exception the earth, or the New Jerusalem."[6]

Ezekiel envisions a future day when there will be a restoration of the earth to the sinless perfection of the garden of Eden (Ezek. 36:35). In that future day the waste places of the earth will become "like Eden . . . the garden of the Lord" (Isa. 51:3). Paradise will result not only in the restoration of the earth, but it will be a day of joy, thanksgiving, and music (Isa. 51:3). The fall of man through the first Adam demands a restoration of all things by the Last Adam, Jesus Christ.

The continuity of the present paradise with the final abode of the redeemed and the restoration of all things is seen in the promise to the overcomers at the church in Ephesus: "To him who overcomes, I will grant to eat of the tree of life which is in the Paradise of God" (Rev. 2:7). References to the "river of the water of life" (Rev. 22:1), the final destruction of Satan (Rev. 20:10), and the reversal of suffering and death (Rev. 21:4) all point to the final restoration of paradise on the renewed earth.[7]

THE INTERMEDIATE HEAVEN

Paradise is described as the dwelling place of believers between death and the resurrection. Christ promised the repentant thief on the cross, "Truly I say to you, today you shall be with Me in Paradise" (Luke 23:43). This is the temporary home of believers prior to receiving their resurrection bodies and living in the new heaven and the new earth (although, as mentioned earlier, there is a continuity in the term "paradise" between Eden and the final abode of believers). It is sometimes referred to as "the intermediate heaven."[8]

Christ's promise to the repentant thief is significant. The promise is a denial of the false doctrines of soul sleep and purgatory. The repentant thief had no works to present to the Lord, only his simple but sincere faith that Jesus was indeed the Christ of God. Yet Jesus promised him that on that very day he would be with the Lord in paradise. "Today" stands in the emphatic position in the Greek text. There would be no interlude for the repentant thief, no waiting, no secondary category of holding before he could enter heaven. Today. When his head dropped in death, his soul and spirit would enter the glories of paradise with the Lord Jesus!

What a glorious truth this promise holds for believers. There is no confusion or question about the destiny of departed loved ones. They are in paradise with the Lord.

Paul yearned for heaven, exclaiming, "I am hard-pressed from both directions, having the desire to depart and be with Christ, for that is very much better" (Phil. 1:23). Paul's desire was strong; the word "desire" stands in the emphatic position. He knew that the moment he left this earthly life, he would be with Christ. That would be "very much better." Again Paul's comments are emphatic and strong. There was no comparison between Paul being with Christ in paradise and being on the old earth.

Although believers will not receive their resurrection bodies until the rapture, it is apparent that believers will have bodies in the intermediate state in heaven. At the transfiguration, Moses and Elijah appeared with Christ to James, Peter, and John (Matt. 17:3–4). The fact that they were seen as the prophets bears testimony to their corporeity. They appeared in bodily form.

In the story of Lazarus and the rich man (Luke 16:19–31), the rich man recognized Abraham and Lazarus. How could he have identified them? He would have had to see them in a physical form. Lazarus is pictured reclining, banquet style, next to Abraham, indicating he was there in physical form (v. 23).

When the believers are martyred during the tribulation, they appear in heaven, crying for justice: "How long, O Lord, holy and true, will You refrain from judging and avenging our blood on those who dwell on the earth?" (Rev. 6:10). Although they are called "souls" (v. 9), the term refers to the entire person, including a physical body (cf. Acts 2:41). They are given robes and told that they should rest for a while. From this we learn that in the intermediate heaven, believers think, know, and remember the former life, and they wear clothing. It indicates there is continuity between the person they were on earth and the person they are in the intermediate heaven. They have bodies as well as minds.

THE NEW HEAVEN AND THE NEW EARTH

The new heaven and the new earth are the final destiny of believers. John received a vision of the new heaven and the new earth coming down from God out of heaven (Rev. 21:1). John went on to describe the realm of the new heaven and the new earth as well as the New Jerusalem. These will be the final destiny and dwelling place of believers throughout eternity. The explanation on the new heaven and the new earth will be developed later.

From this study we learn that the word "heaven" is used in several different ways. The focus of our study will be heaven as the dwelling place of God.

These and other passages also provide us with the wonderful assurance that upon death the believer goes immediately into the presence of Christ in heaven, a realm far better than this earth. It is the preferable life. Paul says he prefers "rather to be absent from the body and to be at home with the Lord" (2 Cor. 5:8). "To be at home" means "to be one among his own people."[9] Heaven is our true home.

And believers have a continuity with their earthly life, both in knowledge and in physical form. They are recognizable and physically identifiable. These wonderful words should remove any fear, any question, and any doubt concerning the destiny of believers at death. We have a strong assurance of our future.

THE NEW JERUSALEM

On one of our trips to Israel, when Helen and I were in Jerusalem, we spoke to a native resident of Jerusalem. "You think this is a holy city?!" he exclaimed. "You will find it is a very unholy city."

Present Jerusalem is certainly a city in turmoil, with Jews and Arabs in constant conflict. But a new Jerusalem is coming where there will no longer be turmoil and warfare. There will be peace—and beauty—and fellowship.

Jesus promised that He was going to prepare a new home for us: "In My Father's house are many dwelling places; if it were not so, I would have told you; for I go to prepare a place for you" (John 14:2). Jesus was referring to the New Jerusalem, described in Revelation 3:12 and 21:2, and He promised, "If I go and prepare a place for you, I will come again and receive you to Myself, that where I am *there* you may be also" (John 14:3, italics added). Jesus will return to take us with Him that we may live with Him forever in the city He has prepared for us. What a glorious future!

The writer of Hebrews also tells us the heavenly Jerusalem will be the place of residence for God Himself, the Lord Jesus, angels, church age believers, and Old Testament saints (Heb. 12:22–24). All believers will have a home in the New Jerusalem; but, as we will see later, the new earth will also be the dwelling place of believers for all eternity. Even as some people today have a home in the city and a second home in the country, perhaps in eternity we will live both in the New Jerusalem and on the new earth.

The New Jerusalem is seen coming down out of heaven (Rev. 21:2). Some believe it hovers over the earth, while others see it descending to the earth itself. Probably the latter is true, since the normal language would suggest that "I saw the holy city, new Jerusalem, coming down out of heaven from God, made ready as a bride adorned for her husband" (Rev. 21:2). Further, what is the point of the New Jerusalem coming down to the earth? It reveals that God again will have fellowship with mankind as when He walked with Adam in the garden of Eden (Gen. 2:15f.). Revelation 21:3 indicates that God will fellowship with the redeemed in eternity: "Behold, the tabernacle of God is among men, and He will dwell among them, and they shall be His people, and God Himself will be among them." The gap that separated the holy and righteous God from sinful humanity has been bridged through the atoning sacrifice of Jesus Christ. Hence, in eternity God will dwell intimately with redeemed mankind.

The New Jerusalem will radiate the glory of God (Rev. 21:10–11). The brilliance and glory "refers to the shining radiance which comes from the presence and glory of God."[10] The brilliance of the city, described "like a very costly stone, as a stone of crystal-clear jasper" (Rev. 21:11), could refer to a diamond; it is an opaque stone that "will connect the light of the heavenly city with God its Maker."[11] The brilliance of the city will continually remind the inhabitants of the presence of the glory of God. He will dwell with His people.

Whether it's designing businesses or home residences, architects always enjoy seeing the outcome of their blueprints—the final product. I worked as a residential architect for several years, and it was always intensely satisfying to see a finished home after the final piece of siding and soffit was hung. But imagine how we all will feel—the excitement—when we see the most magnificent buildings—in fact, a city—ready to be inhabited!

The city known as "the New Jerusalem" is described as a cube, 1,500 miles long, wide, and high (Rev. 21:16). "If we take that literally," Pastor Erwin Lutzer writes, "heaven will be composed of 396,000 stories (at twenty feet per story), each having an area as big as one half the size of the United States! Divide that into separate condominiums, and you have plenty of room for all who have been redeemed by God since the beginning of time."[12] But some may be fearful of such a large city—how would we find anyone in a city of that magnitude? Lutzer's answer: "You need not fear that you will be lost in the crowd; nor need you fear being stuck on the thousandth floor when all of the activity is in the downstairs lounge. All you will need to do is to decide where you would like to be, and you will be there!"[13]

The wall surrounding the city is 216 feet high or wide (Rev. 21:17). It is not entirely clear whether this refers to the height or thickness of the wall. Probably it refers to the thickness of the wall, as Ezekiel also measured its thickness (cf. Ezek. 40:5; 42:20).[14] In this case, the wall would be a reminder that the city is protected—although it would be symbolic since in the eternal state there will be no evil.

The wall of the city has twelve gates, inscribed with the names of the twelve tribes of Israel; twelve angels stand guard at the gates (Rev. 21:12). The twelve angels "function as watchmen to reinforce the impression of security (Isa. 62:6; cf. 2 Chron. 8:14)."[15] Three gates face east, three gates face north, three gates face the south, and three gates face the west (Rev. 21:13).

The city has twelve foundation stones, with the names of the twelve apostles of the Lamb inscribed on them (Rev. 21:14). Since the apostles are the foundation of the church (Eph. 2:20), this is a reminder that the church—the aggregate of believers from Pentecost until the rapture—are also inhabitants of the city.

The jasper wall, dazzling like a diamond, continually reflects the glory of God (Rev. 21:18). Motorists cannot look at the rising sun thirty minutes after daybreak; its sharp rays create a harsh, blinding glare. Drivers heading toward the sunrise must slow down. If we cannot look at the brilliance of the sun, how much more will the New Jerusalem radiate the glory of God? The city, the "buildings, towers, or roofs seen from outside the city" are "pure gold" (Rev. 21:18), suggesting it is "so pure that it is transparent."[16] The golden streets similarly radiate God's glory (v. 21). The foundation stones of the city are adorned with twelve precious stones, emphasizing the beauty and brilliance of the city. It all redounds to the glory of God. Each of the twelve gates is a pearl (v. 21).

Every detail of the city reflects and portrays the greatness, magnificence, and beauty of the Lord. It creates an aura, an awe at the majesty of God. And the wonder of wonders is that we will enjoy eternity, basking in the illuminating presence of the glory of God.

HEAVEN AS A KINGDOM

Heaven is described as a kingdom numerous times in Scripture; it is the eternal kingdom Christ will inaugurate at His second coming. As Daniel explained the dream to Nebuchadnezzar, "In the days of those kings the God of heaven will set up a kingdom which will never be destroyed, and that kingdom will not be left for another people; it will crush and put an end to all these kingdoms, but it will itself endure forever" (Dan. 2:44). The phrases, "never be destroyed . . . endure forever," are reminders that the kingdom exceeds the thousand years of the millennium. The kingdom is eternal. It is heaven's rule on earth.

God gave Daniel a vision that the prophet recounted: "I kept looking in the night visions, and behold, with the clouds of heaven One like a Son of Man was coming, and He came up to the Ancient of Days and was presented before Him. And to Him was given dominion, glory and a kingdom, that all the peoples, nations and men of every language might serve Him. His dominion is an everlasting dominion which will not pass away; and His kingdom is one which will not be destroyed" (Dan. 7:13–14). The statements, "everlasting dominion which will not pass away . . . which will not be destroyed" once more are a reminder of the eternality of Christ's kingdom. It is heaven on earth—on the *new earth.*

A BETTER COUNTRY: OUR HOMELAND

As Americans we proudly sing, "My country 'tis of Thee, sweet land of liberty. . . ." We are proud to be Americans; our country has a great history as a place of refuge and freedom for those who have been persecuted for their faith. Yet most Americans do not have their origin in America. Some 15 percent of Americans have a German background, while about 11 percent have an Irish background. Others have ancestors who came from other European countries. Those are the countries that reflect the background of most Americans (though increasingly immigrants come from Latin America, Asia, the Middle East, and India).

My wife and I made numerous trips to Europe. But on our first trip, after we had spent some time in Germany mingling and interacting with the people, I suddenly turned to Helen and said, "Now I know why I am the way I am." I was in the country of my origin, and I felt comfortable interacting socially with the people. I understood their characteristics and mannerisms, and they unquestionably understood mine.

That familiarity reflects a basic meaning of heaven. One of the rich, colorful words describing heaven is the word *patrida*. The writer of Hebrews reminds us that people like Abraham and Sarah were aliens on this earth. Their sojourn on earth ended in a foreign land. Their hearts were elsewhere. They were "seeking a country [*patrida*] of their own" (Heb. 11:14). They "desire a better country, that is, a heavenly one" (Heb. 11:16).

These concise comments and this singular word *patrida* open a new vista of understanding about heaven. The word has a familiar meaning. It means "fatherland, homeland, home town, one's own part of the country."[17] The word is related to *pater,* meaning "father." Hence, *patrida* has a family meaning. This is where one's family lives. It reflects the family's culture, language, habits. *It is home.* Does that excite you? It should. It is a reminder that we will be with *family* in our *familiar, family home* for all eternity. We will be with family in heaven. We will be home!

The family heritage meaning is also reflected in Luke 2:4 when Joseph left Galilee and went to Bethlehem at the command of Caesar Augustus for the census because Joseph was of the "house and family (*patrias*) of David." Joseph went to his roots at the census taking. Bethlehem was the place of his origin, his ancestry, his home. *Patrias* refers to "ancestral descent."[18] It is where one's ancestors lived.

The word *patrida* is used to describe Galilee as Jesus' homeland. What was Galilee? It was where Jesus lived from infancy until adulthood, when He began His public ministry. It was where He lived with His mother and Joseph and His siblings. It was the familiar locale. It was where He worked in construction with Joseph. The Galileans were known to Him; He lived among them and fellowshiped with them. They were His people.

Patrida means one's hometown. Jesus came to His hometown (probably Capernaum at this time) and taught the parables (Matt. 13:54). It was the town where He was familiar with the people, their language, and their customs (cf. Mk. 6:1, 4). He knew the people, their mannerisms, their culture.

What do you think of when you think of "home" on this earth? Perhaps it is the town where you were born and lived as a youth. Perhaps it is where you lived the majority of your married years. Recently, my sister, Anne, and I drove to the town of Morris in Manitoba, where I was born and where both of us lived in our early years. We drove up and down the streets, reminiscing about our life in the town and the association with family and friends. It was an emotional time. It was where we had roots. It had been our early home.

HEAVEN, OUR TRUE HOME

What is home? It is where you are familiar with the people, their social life, their customs, their spiritual life. You know them. *You feel comfortable; you feel at home there.*

That is heaven! It is our true home. That is where we will be re-united with our believing loved ones and ancestors. We will be *totally comfortable* in those surroundings, enjoying the fellowship, the inter-action, the discussions . . .

When I took my son Jeremy to Germany and Austria, we visited the sites that were special to Helen and me, particularly the town of Enns, the oldest city in Austria. We mingled with the people and sat in the town square of Mondsee, watching the people strolling in the square, sitting in outdoor cafes, visiting with their family and friends. I invited Jeremy to sit on the favorite bench where Helen and I sat in the town square, facing the old church where Maria Von Trapp was married in *The Sound of Music.* We watched—old and young, teenagers, middle-aged and elderly strolling—not going anywhere, simply enjoying a re-laxing evening. It was *feierabend*—"celebration of the evening," which comes every evening after the workday is over. It is the time to relax, rest, and enjoy family and friends in social life.

Children were playing hide and seek, boys were kicking a soccer ball without a specific game plan. A little girl was riding her scooter. "Where's her mother?" exclaimed Jeremy. She was nowhere to be seen. People weren't anxious for their little ones. They felt secure; there was no sense of crime. It was *feierabend*—people were resting and fellowshiping.

Eventually a group of men and women marched into the square, playing "oompapa" music. They sat down in the square and soon be-gan to entertain the people sitting in the square with pleasant, old-fashioned music. We sat, observed, listened, and were captivated by the lifestyle. I felt at home. Although this had been new to me in visiting Austria, it was not new to me from home. I grew up in a home where the evenings were spent with music; my father would play the violin, and my mother, sister, or brother played the piano. Strauss waltzes! My father loved the melodious music of Johann Strauss—and so did the rest of us. So Austria became home to me.

The people in Austria and Germany enjoy a relaxed lifestyle, spending considerable time in fellowship with family and friends. Jeremy quickly grasped the cultural model of Austria and also Germany. When we returned home he exclaimed, "Dad, you've ruined me!" He had grasped the culture, connected with it, and loved it!

Recently my son Terry and I visited the German Mennonite villages south of Elblag (Elbing), Poland, in what was formerly northeastern Germany. Helen's ancestors and my ancestors lived there in the 1500s until the late 1700s. That represents Helen's homeland and my homeland. We found an old Mennonite cemetery with stone markers dating from the 1700s. On the front of the monument was the name of the person but on the backside, engraved in the stone, was the testimony of the person's faith. Tears streamed down my face as I read the humble, sincere statements of faith. I'm eager to meet my family members who lived there. I'm eager to talk with them and have fellowship with them in heaven. It will be *home.*

WHAT WE LONG FOR

What are you looking for and longing for? In America, people sometimes long for the wrong things—and what they really want (although they don't know it) and what they really need will remain elusive to them. Many think they need another car, a vacation home, the newest items in technology. They think the latest fashions in the shopping centers will satisfy their longings. They won't.

The longing that God has placed in our hearts is for heaven, a better place, a better country. But more specifically, it is a country of our ancestry. It is our *fatherland.* It is where we will meet believing ancestors and converse and excitedly fellowship with them. We will enjoy becoming connected with *our people,* who do things in a familiar way, who speak a familiar language. It is a people with whom we will be *totally comfortable.*

Are you looking for the better country? Are you looking for your fatherland, your homeland, your home town? That is heaven! That is the deep longing in your heart—and only heaven—our family home—will satisfy that longing.

What Is the TRANSITION to HEAVEN?

William Randolph Hearst, the newspaper magnate of yesteryear, so feared death that he prohibited anyone from mentioning the word or speaking about death. He also demanded that the lights be continually kept on because of his inordinate fear of death.

For every living person, death remains the greatest dilemma. Neither one's wealth nor status can prevent death's invasion. It will capture every man and woman. As someone has said, "Death is all inclusive—it's one out of one." People of the world fear death because they cannot avoid it.

Yet Jesus made the startling statement that we need not fear death: "Do not fear those who kill the body but are unable to kill the soul; but rather fear Him who is able to destroy both soul and body in hell" (Matt. 10:28). Jesus reminded us that the eternal destiny of the soul is more important than the existence of the body in this life.

How is that? Through Jesus' death and resurrection He has destroyed the power of death. Through the incarnation, Jesus took on humanity, died an atoning death for the sins of the world, and thereby conquered the adversary who held the power of death. Hebrews 2:14 reminds us, "He Himself likewise also partook of the same [humanity], that through death He might render powerless him who had the power of death, that is, the devil." The term translated as "render powerless" means "to render inoperative, to nullify, to make idle or ineffective, to render impotent as though no longer existing."[1] What a phenomenal truth! The writer of Hebrews encourages us to not fear death because Jesus Christ has destroyed the power of death as though it no longer existed. Those who were enslaved to the fear of death have been set free (Heb. 2:15). That refers to us! Followers of Jesus have been set free from the fear of death.

Those who have taken the Scriptures at face value can know the unbelievable peace of God when the human experience of death comes their way. My mother sat with my father the hour he was dying of tuberculosis. As she read Psalm 23 to him, my father responded, "How nice!" Then she read John 5:24, a favorite verse of his. He knew the peace of God, and in that tranquility he passed into the presence of the eternal God.

OUR EXISTENCE CONTINUES

Believers do not cease to exist at death. Many have a misunderstanding of the meaning of death. Death is not cessation of existence; death is separation of the body from the soul and spirit (James 2:26).[2] The body temporarily goes into the grave, awaiting the resurrection, but the person—complete with all thoughts, memory, and personality—continues. There is no interruption in the believer's continued existence. Upon death the person's soul and spirit are immediately in the presence of God in heaven (2 Cor. 5:6, 8)

This is evident in Stephen's stoning. Stephen's body expired (Acts 7:60), but Jesus received Stephen's spirit into heaven (Acts 7:59).

Stephen's existence continued uninterrupted. Jesus Himself in His death reflected this truth. In His earthly body "He breathed His last," but in His spirit He was immediately in the Father's presence (Luke 23:46). He was at that moment in the paradise of heaven (Luke 23:43).

Some teach the doctrine of "soul sleep," the notion that the soul as well as the body die, and both body and soul await the resurrection. Still others believe that the entire person—body, soul, and spirit—is annihilated at death and ceases to exist. These are false doctrines. Scriptures such as Luke 16 teach that both believer and unbeliever continue immediately after death. Existence continues at death for the believer in a fuller, and more fulfilling, way. Death should hold no fear for the believer.

WE SHALL NEVER DIE

Jesus made a most provocative statement concerning death. He said, "I am the resurrection and the life; he who believes in Me shall live even if he dies, and everyone who lives and believes in Me will never die" (John 11:25–26). It almost sounds contradictory, yet Jesus was referring to the distinction between the material and immaterial part of man. The first statement recognizes the death of the physical body; it goes into the grave. But the second statement speaks of the spiritual nature of man, the soul and spirit. They never die. The one who lives and believes in Jesus Christ as his sin-bearer will never die spiritually. The body goes into the earth, awaiting the resurrection, but the soul and spirit—the real essence of the person—go home to the Father in heaven. Jesus stated this in the strongest terms, using the double negative in the Greek text, which can be translated: "Everyone who is living and believing in me shall *not never—by no means*—die."

Jesus' words are a strong reminder and encouragement that in the event of death, the real person does not die. The believer goes home to the Lord. Solomon also recognized this, saying, "then the dust will return to the earth as it was, and the spirit will return to God who gave it" (Eccl. 12:7).

Paul provides a startling statement to the reader: "But now has been revealed by the appearing of our Savior Christ Jesus, who abolished death and brought life and immortality to light through the gospel" (2 Tim. 1:10). Abolished death! Those are truly stunning words. We see death all around us. We read about death daily in the newspapers. We see it on television. We stand at a gravesite and weep. Now the Scriptures tell us that Christ has abolished death. The statement is strong. "Abolished" means "to render inoperative, to make inactive, to annul."[3] The statement of Scripture draws a strong contrast: On the one hand, Christ has abolished death; on the other hand, He has brought life and immortality.[4]

This statement is a further reminder that death will never overtake the believer. Immortality! Think of it. "Immortality" (*athanasian*) means precisely what a person anticipates: "that which is not subject to death."[5] Death is gone, banished—forever. Believers take on *immortality*. Although this mortal, earthly body is laid to rest in the grave, the real person, the soul and spirit, continue on, uninterrupted as the believer is transported into glory. There the believer continues in genuine, real life and *immortality*.

DEATH IS AN ADVANTAGE

Paul had no fear of death. It didn't matter to Paul whether he lived or died. If he was living, it meant living in fellowship and service for Christ; if he died, it was advantageous. Paul made the startling statement, "To die is gain" (Phil. 1:21). How is death "gain"? "Gain" speaks of "advantage" and "profit . . . Paul says that for him to live is Christ, and therefore death, in which this life finds fulfillment in sight, is advantage or gain."[6] In what way? For Paul, death "could not in any way separate him from Christ (see Rom. 8:38–39). . . . in death there was a continuing relationship with Christ. Life which is centered on Christ is thus not destroyed by death; it is only increased and enriched by death."[7]

Death prevents us from staying in this sinful, suffering world of sickness. Erwin Lutzer reminds us that "only death can give us the gift of eternity. . . . Death [escorts us] into the presence of God. . . . Death might temporarily take our friends from us, but only to introduce us to that land in which there are no good-byes."[8]

What a wonderful, blessed truth. The believer living in fellowship with Christ transitions into a better, fuller, more wonderful relationship with Christ. The relationship is never separated; it is enhanced. It reminds me of an occasion when, as a young pastor, I spoke to an elderly, godly man from California, who, with his wife, visited the church I pastored. When I saw him alone, I asked him about his wife. He exclaimed, "Oh, she has gone home to be with the Lord. And I am so happy for her, that she is in the presence of Jesus, that I almost feel guilty that I'm not sorrowing more!"

I was startled at the man's response, but he had the biblical perspective. At death the believer enters into a fuller, more wonderful relationship with Christ.

OUR TENT IS TAKEN DOWN

My wife and I enjoyed camping; in fact, when we got married, it was Helen who had all the camping equipment. We loved going to Banff and Jasper in the Rockies of western Canada. We'd set up our eight-foot-by-eight-foot tent at our camping spot, but when our temporary journey to Banff ended; we pulled up the stakes, folded the tent, and headed for home. Banff was only a temporary visit; it wasn't home. Our real home, our permanent home, was elsewhere. We enjoyed our visit to Banff, but we always looked forward to going back to our real home.

That is the imagery in Scripture. Paul says, "For we know that if the earthly tent which is our house is torn down, we have a building from God, a house not made with hands, eternal in the heavens" (2 Cor. 5:1). When we depart this earth for heaven, we leave behind our temporary dwelling and receive our permanent dwelling, "a building from God, a house not made with hands." The "house" describes "the glorified body of the departed Christian," note Gingrich and Danker.[9] "The earthly body is a tent which can be dismantled. . . . But then we have a house from God which is not made with hands, which is eternal, and which is ready in heaven."[10] The fact that the same root word *oikos* ("house") is used for both the body in this life and the new body in heaven is a reminder that immediately upon death the believer receives a greater body than he now possesses; even though it is prior to the resurrection when we will receive a glorified body.

The tent is a reminder that we are on a pilgrimage, like visiting a foreign country. A tent is temporary. After a brief sojourn on earth, we pull up stakes and trade in our tent for a heavenly home. We weren't made to live in a tent forever; we were made for a mansion.

WE DEPART FOR OUR NEW HOME

Paul had conflicting emotions; on the one hand he sensed the necessity of staying and serving the Philippian believers (Phil. 1:24) but inwardly there was a strong emotional "desire to depart and be with Christ, for that is very much better" (Phil. 1:23). "Depart" (*analuo*) means "to unloose, to undo. It is used of loosening a ship from its moorings."[11] It means to lift the anchor and travel to another destination. When people sail away, people on shore wave good-bye amid tears . . . but at the ship's destination, people are eagerly shouting and waving welcome!

Why does a crew member on a ship lift an anchor? To depart to a better destination. At death, the believer lifts anchor and leaves for the better destination—heaven.

In Heaven...

1. Our existence continues.
2. We shall never die.
3. We are in our new home.
4. Angels will escort us.
5. Christ will welcome us.
6. We will be with Christ.
7. We will be reunited with loved ones.
8. We will be home.
9. We will be where Jesus wants us to be.

As I visited my friend Skip in the hospital, with peaceful composure he simply said, "I'll see you on the other side, pastor." Not long afterwards, with his wife at his side, he said, "Cheryl, I'm going now. I love you. Good-bye." And Skip entered heaven. He had departed for his new home.

When Moses and Elijah appeared on the Mount of Transfiguration, they "were speaking of His [Jesus'] departure which He was about to accomplish at Jerusalem" (Luke 9:31). The language is picturesque. "Departure" (*exodus*) is the word describing Israel's departure from Egypt for their new and better home in the Promised Land.[12] What is the significance? The Hebrew people were departing from a land where they endured persecution, suffering, and slavery for the Promised Land, a land flowing with milk and honey. Their departure was taking them away from trials and bringing them into a land of triumph.

Peter used the same expression, "departure," to refer to "laying aside of my earthly dwelling" (2 Peter 1:14, 15). Josephus also uses it "for riding out ... for setting off."[13] Where? To the believer's new home! It pictures a journey to the believer's home in heaven.

What is death? It is our departure for our real home! It means we leave the troubles of this fallen earth and enter into the joy of our new home, our real home.

ANGELS WILL ESCORT US

When my brother-in-law lay dying, he exclaimed, "Who are all those people?" Only my sister and the medical doctor were present with him. Then I realized the reality: Angels had come to escort him home, and he was already seeing the people who were welcoming him into heaven!

When Lazarus died, he "was carried away by the angels to Abraham's bosom" (Luke 16:22a). The angels are God's royal attendants, giving the believer a grand entrance into the royal court of the Lord Jesus! They carry the believer "to Abraham's bosom," a reference to "the place of honor at a banquet."[14]

CHRIST WILL WELCOME US

When the Sanhedrin had Stephen stoned to death, Stephen "gazed intently into heaven and saw the glory of God, and Jesus standing at the right hand of God" (Acts 7:55). Jesus is seated at the right hand of the Father in heaven (Heb. 1:3). But now Jesus rose from His seat and stood to welcome His servant into heaven! What a glorious entrance into heaven's portals!

Helen and I were rarely separated during our married years, but on a few occasions one of us took a trip alone. When her parents celebrated their golden wedding anniversary, she traveled to Canada alone to the celebration. My sons and I anticipated her homecoming, so we decorated the house with colorful streamers and charted the days until her return on a giant graph on the wall. What a celebration and reunion when Helen arrived home! We were there to meet her and rejoice in her homecoming. But how much grander will be our entrance into heaven when Christ Himself is there to welcome us!

We will look on Him who loved us and gave His life for us so that we could live in glory forever with Him and with our loved ones. We will see His face. First John 3:2 says, "We know that when He appears, we will be like Him, because we will see Him just as He is." As Rogers and Rogers write, "This likeness of man redeemed and perfected to God is the likeness of the creature reflecting the glory of the Creator."[15]

What a phenomenal truth! Our tired, weak, mortal bodies will be changed into incorruptible, strong, immortal bodies like the body of Christ. And we will see Him. He will be radiant with the *shekinah* glory of God reflecting from His person. We will bask in the glorious light of His presence forever.

WE WILL BE WITH CHRIST

Jesus spoke remarkable words to the thief on the cross. He was a convicted thief; he had nothing to offer God. He had lived his life apart from God, and now he was moments away from facing the righteous and holy God. What could he do? What could he say? He had nothing. He simply said, "Jesus, remember me when You come in Your kingdom" (Luke 23:42). But he displayed a simple, humble faith, and for that Jesus promised him, "Truly I say to you, today you shall be with Me in Paradise" (Luke 23:43). At that moment the thief was suffering agony, hanging on the cross, having been lacerated with the brutal flogging that Christ also had received. But in moments the pain and misery would transition to unspeakable glory and joy. Not some time in the future but this very day . . . only moments away . . . he would breath celestial air. As Oswald Sanders has said, "The moment we take the last breath on earth, we take our first breath in heaven."[16]

Jesus' words are pointed and powerful. "Today" stands in the emphatic position in the text. "Today," this very day, the repentant thief would experience the bliss of heaven. His body would go into the grave, but spiritually, in his essence as a person, he would enter heaven.

The thief had heard Christ's words on the cross and came to recognize He was indeed the Messiah who would usher in the glorious kingdom. So Jesus promised the thief that he would indeed be with Him. "With Me"(*meta*) is a beautiful phrase that emphasizes a close association—genuine, close fellowship, the fellowship of friends and companions in company with one another.[17] The one who had run with thieves and robbers would now have an eternity of close fellowship with the Savior Himself. Revelation 21:3 depicts the same picture. The same preposition (*meta*), translated as "with" in this passage, is translated as "among" in Revelation 21:3: "The tabernacle of God is among men, and He will dwell among them, and they shall be His people, and God Himself will be among them." Think of it. God Himself will be in a close relationship with His people. That is what we can expect the moment we close our eyes for the last time on this earth. We will see the Lord Himself. He will greet us. We will be in close, wonderful fellowship with Him forever.

Jesus made an interesting statement in John 17:24 when He prayed to the Father: "Father, I desire that they also, whom You have given Me, be with Me where I am, so that they may see My glory . . ." Think of it! What is Jesus' prayer? What is His desire? For us to be with Him where He is. Where is He? He is in heaven. Where does He want us to be? With Him in heaven. That should give enormous comfort and peace to us when a believing loved one departs this life. Jesus' prayer for them is answered. They have gone to be with Him, and that is His desire.

WE WILL BE REUNITED WITH LOVED ONES

Following His resurrection, Jesus met the disciples "and greeted them" (Matt. 28:9). The Greek text is emphatic: "And behold, Jesus met them saying, 'Rejoice!'" Jesus' greeting is strong and enthusiastic, "Rejoice, be glad . . . greetings!"[18]

We will excitedly greet one another at that glorious reunion with our believing loved ones. The very moment earth's door closes and heaven's door opens—at that very moment—there will be an excited, joyful, and exuberant reunion.

On one occasion Helen escorted her blind brother to Austria for three weeks of eye treatment while I stayed at home. As the day of her return grew closer, my sons and I became excited as we prepared for her return. What an exciting moment it was when I saw my Helen again! The sparkle in her eyes, the smile on her face—what a joyful, happy moment it was to see Helen again! We hugged and hugged and looked at each other and talked and talked. This is a miniature portrayal of the glorious, exciting reunion of loved ones as they enter heaven.

Scripture is also clear that there will be recognizable reunion with family members immediately at death. When Abraham died, "he was gathered to his people" (Gen. 25:8; cf. 25:17; 35:29; 49:29, 33). The picture is further illuminated in Matthew 8:11 with Abraham reclining in the kingdom with Isaac and Jacob—his son and grandson. Family reunion! For believers, death brings a joyful reunion with believing family members. What a prospect!

THE POWER OF DEATH IS DESTROYED

On December 21, 1899, D. L. Moody awoke from sleep early in the morning and began to speak: "Earth recedes; heaven opens before me." His son was at his bedside and thought he was dreaming and attempted to rouse him. "No, this is no dream, Will," Mr. Moody replied.

"It is beautiful. It is like a trance. If this is death, it is sweet. There is no valley here. God is calling me, and I must go."

Mr. Moody continued to talk as if from another world. "Then it seemed as though he saw beyond the veil, for he exclaimed, 'This is my triumph; this is my Coronation Day! I have been looking forward to it for years.' Then his face lit up, and he said, in a voice of joyful rapture, 'Dwight! Irene! I see the children's faces!'"—referring to the two little grandchildren God had taken from his life in the past year.[19] Moments later Moody was gone. He had entered heaven.

Christ is destined to reign as king, and in so doing He has authority over every realm and enemy, over Satan and his domain, and over every aspect of nature, including death. The Scripture says, "He must reign until He has put all His enemies under His feet. The last enemy that will be abolished is death" (1 Cor. 15:25–26). Through His death and resurrection, Christ indeed has conquered death. The Scripture says that death will be abolished, meaning He will bring death to an end. It will be no more.

Through Christ's victory we become immortal. Scripture says, "For this perishable must put on the imperishable, and this mortal must put on immortality" (1 Cor. 15:53). That truth will be consummated at the rapture when we receive glorified bodies. Then the prophecy of Isaiah will be fulfilled, "Death is swallowed up in victory" (Isa. 25:8; 1 Cor. 15:54). The term "in victory" is a Semitic phrase meaning "forever, permanently, successfully."[20]

Death had power through sin but Christ conquered sin and death. Hence, Paul exclaims, "O death, where is your victory? O death, where is your sting?" (1 Cor. 15:55). The sting of death is gone. "Sting" is a word that "represents death as a venomous creature, a scorpion, or a hornet which is rendered harmless."[21] Death is destroyed; its power over believers is removed. For this reason we can go through life with peace and strength. Paul said, "Thanks be to God, who gives us the victory through our Lord Jesus Christ. Therefore, my beloved brethren, be steadfast, immovable, always abounding in the work of the Lord, knowing that your toil is not in vain in the Lord" (1 Cor. 15:57–58).

WE WILL BE HOME

When we close our eyes for the last time, we will immediately open our eyes in our new home—our real home. We will truly be "home." The apostle Paul had a preference "rather to be absent from the body and to be at home with the Lord" (2 Cor. 5:8). Some years ago there was a reunion of the living descendants of my maternal grandmother, Maria Schroeder. When we gathered on the college campus for the reunion fellowship and festivities, over two hundred descendants showed up. Some of the relatives I had not seen in many years—and some I had never seen before! What an excitement; what a celebration! Why? Because we were *family*. We were *at home with each other.*

We had much in common—our prized ancestry, our customs, our joking in our unwritten Low German dialect, our united love of music and singing. The joy was reflected in singing the well-known hymns so dear to us all. Tears of joy fell from our faces. We were at home with each other, and yet the emotion, the joy, the laughter, and the tears were reflective of the inner longing for *our ultimate home—heaven!*

Our imagination is strained as we anticipate the excitement, the joy, the greater tears and laughter that will reflect our arrival at our true home.

WE WILL BE WHERE JESUS WANTS US TO BE

Some of the most remarkable words Jesus spoke were from the prayer to His Father. As He anticipated going to the cross and ultimately to the Father, He prayed, "Father, I desire that they also, whom You have given Me, be with Me where I am, so that they may see My glory which You have given Me" (John 17:24).

What was Jesus' request? He was praying that believers in Him would be *with Him*. Where was He going? *To heaven.* Jesus' ultimate prayer for His own people is that they would be in fellowship with Him in heaven forever. This is Jesus' desire, and "it is more than a mere wish. . . . The petition looks for the disciples to be with Jesus in the next world rather than this (cf. 14:3)," wrote Bible commentator Leon Morris.[22]

Jesus wants us to be with Him—and with each other—in His Father's house.

WE WILL ARRIVE SAFELY IN OUR HOME IN HEAVEN

Frances Havergal wrote such beautiful hymns as "Like a River Glorious" and "Take My Life and Let It Be." But Frances did not enjoy good health. She was only forty-three when she faced departure from this world. But her attitude was amazing. "If I am going, it is too good to be true," she exclaimed to her loved ones. She smiled and said, "Splendid to be so near the gates of heaven! I am lost in amazement! There has not failed one word of all His good promises!"

"Shortly afterward, Frances looked up steadfastly as if seeing the Lord. 'For ten minutes we watched that almost visible meeting with her King,' wrote Maria, 'and her countenance was so glad, as if she were already talking to Him! Then she tried to sing, but after one sweet, high note . . . her voice failed and her brother commended her soul into the Redeemer's hand, and she passed away."[23]

When the apostle Paul wrote Second Timothy, he was only a month or two away from being executed by beheading—and he knew it. It was in that circumstance and mental framework that Paul wrote the confident, upbeat words, "The Lord will rescue me from every evil deed, and will bring me safely to His heavenly kingdom; to Him be the glory forever and ever. Amen" (2 Tim. 4:18).

How could Paul be so confident? How could he write these reassuring words? He could write them because there is nothing—absolutely nothing—that can thwart the believer's safe arrival in heaven!

What is your circumstance today? You may be having severe difficulties in life: tragedy, sadness, serious illness. God's people do indeed suffer in this fallen world. Whether because of persecution in the Middle East or because of illness in America—believers suffer. Before we lay down our head the last time, each one of us will suffer in some way.

So what is the significance of Paul's promise? Paul sees death as a *good* thing. The very wording Paul uses, "The Lord will rescue me *from* ("*apo*") every evil deed," means Paul "is assured of the removal *from the presence of* 'every evil work,' and that through death."[24] Death brings release and removal from all evil, every tragedy, and all difficulty. Death is not an enemy. As Lutzer has pointed out, "God prevented Adam and Eve from eternal sinfulness by giving them the gift of death, the ability to exit this life and arrive safely in the wondrous life to come. Death, though it would appear to be man's greatest enemy, would in the end, prove to be his greatest friend. Only through death can we go to God."[25]

Moreover, Paul's promise concludes the Lord "will bring me safely to His heavenly kingdom." The phrase "will bring me safely" (*sosei*) means the Lord will save Paul and rescue him from the troubles of this earth by bringing him home to heaven.[26]

Paul was so excited at the prospect of his safe and certain arrival in heaven that he burst into a doxology: "To Him be the glory forever and ever. Amen." As believers we have no need to fear death. Christ Himself assures us of a safe arrival home in heaven!

OUR PRECISE DAYS ARE APPOINTED

When did Jesus die? At precisely the time the Father had determined. In Egypt the Israelites celebrated the Passover Feast 1,400 years before the time of Christ's earthly life. At that event, on the fourteenth day of Nisan, the Israelites killed the Passover lamb at twilight (Ex. 12:6), which, according to Josephus, was three in the afternoon. Jesus was the fulfillment of the Passover prophecy; the lamb slain on the fourteenth of Nisan foreshadowed the coming of Christ. When did Christ die? On the Passover, the fourteenth of Nisan, at 3:00 p.m., *precisely* the time the Father had ordained (John 19:14; Mark 15:33).

Our day of transition to glory is precisely the day that has been planned by the Father. Job says, "Since his days are determined, the number of his months is with You; and his limits You have set so that he cannot pass" (Job 14:5). Scripture says that not only are our days precisely determined, we cannot live beyond them. When the doctor diagnoses a terminal illness, we can rest at peace that our days have been precisely determined by God. Scripture affirms, "Your eyes have seen my unformed substance; and in your book they were all written the days that were ordained for me, when as yet there was not one of them" (Ps. 139:16). Before we were born, God appointed the precise number of days that we would live.

We can't fathom this, nor should we try. My mother-in-law lived to nearly ninety-three years, but my beloved Helen outlived her only by five years, going home at sixty-five. My father died at forty-eight, but my mother lived until eighty-nine; she was a widow for forty-three years. We don't understand this, and we never will—until we get to glory, and then it won't matter.

The psalmist says, "With Your counsel You will guide me, and afterward receive me to glory" (Ps. 73:24). God directs our lives, all the details, event after event, year after year, and then at precisely the right time, He takes us home. God determines the number of days we spend on earth. They are different for each of us. Some live longer lives, some shorter. Then, at the end of our days, He receives us home, into the brilliance of His heavenly home.

Where Is

HEAVEN?

It is not uncommon to read authors locating heaven somewhere in outer space. They suggest that heaven is beyond our solar system, beyond the distant stars, far in outer space. Probably most people think that heaven is somewhere in the far distance.

Where does the Bible locate heaven? Scripture indicates that heaven is not distant, but rather heaven is *near*. Heaven is in another *realm*.

Perhaps this is a new concept to you, but consider the Scriptures and let them speak. Some Scriptures unquestionably are clearer than others (and it is possible some of these incidents are visions, although it is not stated that they are visions). But I invite you to consider this new thought: Heaven is near—in another realm.

ELISHA SAW ELIJAH GO UP INTO HEAVEN

When God called Elijah home, Elisha saw his master go "up by a whirlwind to heaven" (2 Kings 2:11). It is unlikely that Elisha saw Elijah go far away into the sky. Rather, the inference is that heaven is near; Elisha saw his master enter heaven. Amid the blaze of fiery light, the windstorm carried Elijah into heaven. It appears that Elijah was removed quickly since Elisha "saw Elijah no more" (v. 12). This implies Elisha did not see Elijah for a long period of time. Elijah had passed into heaven —another realm, not obvious to normal viewing.

Similarly, when the servant was fearful because of the invading Syrian army, Elisha prayed that his eyes would be opened. "And the Lord opened the servant's eyes, and he saw; and behold, the mountain was full of horses and chariots of fire all around Elisha" (2 Kings 6:17b). When the Lord pulled back the curtain, a powerful army was nearby! Where had this army come from? Heaven! They did not come from a distant land or from outer space; they came from another realm, normally unseen to the human eye. "The fiery horses and chariots were symbols of the protecting powers of heaven, which surrounded the prophet."[1] Elisha saw into the realm of heaven.

That heaven is near us yet in a different sphere is implied in 2 Kings 6:17 when Elisha prayed that the servant's eyes would be opened; the servant then saw into the new realm, where "the mountain was full of horses and chariots of fire all around Elisha."

How is this explained? "The opening of the eyes signifies elevation into an ecstatic state in which the soul sees things which the bodily eye never can see."[2] While it is true that Elisha saw in another dimension, it is probably better to state that Elisha saw with *both* his physical eyes and spiritual eyes. It was not a vision. Elisha saw "the mountain was full of horses and chariots of fire." The Lord enabled Elisha to see his protective forces surrounding him, forces that were able in a moment to decimate the Syrians.

ISAIAH SAW THE LORD ON HIS THRONE

The words of Isaiah 6:1 are dramatic and forceful. "In the year of King Uzziah's death I saw the Lord sitting on a throne, lofty and exalted, with the train of His robe filling the temple." The language is clear and unequivocal: Isaiah saw into the realm of heaven. The prophet was not asleep and dreaming. "God gave him, when awake, an insight into the invisible world . . . Isaiah is here carried up into heaven."[3] He saw the heavenly temple and the surrounding seraphim. The ensuing description details the scene in heaven around the throne of God (Isa. 6:2ff.). Moreover, Isaiah recognizes he has seen the Lord in heaven, and he is fearful (Isa. 6:5).

At the beginning of the prophet's ministry, the Lord allowed him to see the exalted Lord in heaven, to appropriate a proper perspective, to prepare the prophet for a ministry in which he would fearlessly stand strong against the evils of an apostate nation. And it changed Isaiah's life. The Lord gave him a long and effective ministry. The Lord allowed Isaiah to see into the realm of heaven.

EZEKIEL SAW INTO THE HEAVENLY THRONE ROOM

After Ezekiel was taken into exile in Babylon, the Lord revealed Himself to the prophet. Ezekiel explains, "While I was by the river Chebar among the exiles, the heavens were opened and I saw visions of God" (Ezek. 1:1). "The picture created by Ezekiel's description is of the door being opened into the heavenly throne room of God."[4]

What an astounding picture! When God opens heaven's door, it enables His people to look into heaven as though they were looking through the doorway into another room in a house. Ezekiel saw with his physical eyes, but it probably also involved spiritual insight, enabling Ezekiel to see into the realm of heaven, which was nearby.

NEBUCHADNEZZAR SAW INTO HEAVEN

When God revealed Himself to Nebuchadnezzar in a dream, the Babylonian king became alarmed and told Daniel, "I was looking in the visions in my mind as I lay on my bed, and behold, an angelic watcher, a holy one, descended from heaven" (Dan. 4:13). Daniel acknowledged the validity of what Nebuchadnezzar had seen—he had indeed seen an angel descending from heaven (Dan. 4:23). The fulfillment of the revelation to Nebuchadnezzar was verified when "a voice came from heaven" (Dan. 4:31).

As God revealed to Nebuchadnezzar the judgment that was about to fall on him, God delivered His message through an angel from heaven and later God Himself spoke to Nebuchadnezzar. God was not distant; He was nearby—in another realm.

DANIEL SAW INTO HEAVEN

Daniel recorded the vision he saw when the Lord revealed the climax of the ages to him: "I kept looking in the night visions, and behold, with the clouds of heaven one like a Son of Man was coming . . ." (Dan. 7:13). The picture is graphic. "The word for 'was coming' is a participle depicting Christ, as Daniel looked on, moving into the courtroom before the Ancient of Days."[5] Daniel saw the process, the Son of Man coming down to earth from heaven to establish His kingdom and rule on the earth. Daniel saw into heaven!

Daniel's vision is a reminder that the ultimate heaven will be fulfilled in God's original purpose: to establish the kingdom of His Son on earth where Christ will rule and the triune God will live in fellowship with redeemed humanity for all eternity.

STEPHEN SAW JESUS STANDING NEXT TO GOD

Heaven appears to Christ's followers in the New Testament. The account of Stephen's stoning is also graphic. As Stephen was drawing his last also breath, "he gazed intently into heaven and saw the glory of God, and Jesus standing at the right hand of God" (Acts 7:55). Stephen's gaze was fixated as he exclaimed, "Behold, I see the heavens opened up and the Son of Man standing at the right hand of God" (Acts 7:56). Stephen was looking into heaven! "The heavens opened," indicating that heaven was not distant but nearby, in another realm.

The language was strong and clear as Stephen described what he sees. He saw the blaze of the *shekinah* glory of God. He saw Jesus standing at the right hand of God—which was unique since Jesus had previously taken His seat at the right hand of the Father, His work being completed (Luke 22:69; Eph. 1:20; Col. 3:1). Why was Jesus standing? He was welcoming Stephen into heaven!

What glorious joy and hope must have filled Stephen's heart. On earth he was about to suffer severely, but God would mellow the suffering by giving Stephen a preview of the glory that awaited him. And it was nearby! Jesus was welcoming the faithful servant into heaven.

This is a strong reminder of what awaits every believer departing this old earth. The believer immediately transitions into heaven and is welcomed home by Jesus Himself. The Lord opened the portals of heaven, allowing Stephen to see into the realm of heaven, which would be a strong comfort and encouragement to every believer.

Where is heaven? Heaven is nearby! And from it Jesus welcomes His people into heaven. What a prospect!

PAUL HEARD JESUS SPEAKING FROM HEAVEN

As Saul (Paul) was traveling on his way to Damascus to persecute the Christians, the Lord confronted him: "Suddenly a light from heaven flashed around him; and he fell to the ground and heard a voice saying to him, 'Saul, Saul, why are you persecuting Me?'" (Acts 9:3b–4). A light from heaven penetrated to Saul, followed by Jesus speaking to Saul from heaven (v. 5). Heaven was close enough that Saul could converse with Jesus, even though Saul was on earth and Jesus was in heaven.

Where was heaven? Not far away; it was nearby but in another realm.

PETER TALKED WITH THE LORD

When Peter had difficulty leaving the Levitical law, the Lord revealed Himself to Peter. The apostle was on the rooftop of a house in Joppa when "he fell into a trance; and he saw the sky opened up, and an object like a great sheet coming down, lowered by four corners to the ground" (Acts 10:10b–11). The Lord was about to teach Peter that there is no partiality with God. The language of what occurred is explicit. Peter saw *(theoreo)* the event, theorizing what happened. He was seeing heaven opening to him. The verbs "saw" and "opened" are graphic, indicating Peter watched the process as ongoing; it was not a sudden event.

It is a picturesque scene, as Peter is continuously seeing what is occurring. Heaven is opening to him! God is speaking to him! Peter had his private, verbal audience with the Lord. And the Lord was nearby in heaven!

JOHN WATCHES AND HEARS
JESUS' TRIUMPHANT RETURN

In announcing the destruction of commercial Babylon, John recorded, "I saw another angel coming down from heaven" (Rev. 18:1). "Saw"[6] describes the ongoing event of John continuously seeing the angel as he descended from heaven.

As John described the triumphant return of Jesus Christ, he wrote, "After these things I heard something like a loud voice of a great multitude in heaven, saying, 'Hallelujah! Salvation and glory and power belong to our God" (Rev. 19:1). John was on earth, but he heard the great multitude chorus the chant of victory from heaven! How far is heaven

How Witnesses Describe Heaven's Location

1. Elisha saw Elijah go up into heaven.

2. Isaiah saw the Lord on His throne.

3. Ezekiel saw into the heavenly throne room.

4. Nebuchadnezzar saw into heaven.

5. Daniel saw into heaven.

6. Stephen saw Jesus standing next to God.

7. Paul heard Jesus speaking from heaven.

8. Peter talked with the Lord.

9. John watches and hears Jesus' triumphant return.

10. Jesus said heaven is near.

11. Jesus watched heaven come near.

if John can hear the multitude in heaven rejoicing at the impending victory of Christ's triumphant return to earth? It is near.

John not only heard the songs of triumph, but he saw the worship in heaven in anticipation of Christ's glorious reign on earth (Rev. 19:4ff.). John saw the twenty-four elders and the four living creatures prostrate before God, who sat on the throne. Then John heard the exhortation from heaven to give praise to God (Rev. 19:5). But John heard more—"the voice of a great multitude and like the sound of many waters and like the sound of mighty peals of thunder" (Rev. 19:6). It was dramatic and loud—a call to the people to rejoice in anticipation of Christ's reign.

How could John see this? How could he hear the voices from heaven? God allowed John to see into heaven and hear the multitudes in heaven praising the impending reign of Christ. Heaven could not be distant; it was nearby!

JESUS SAID HEAVEN IS NEAR

While on earth Jesus verified the nearness of heaven when He told Nathanael, "Truly, truly, I say to you, you will see the heavens opened and the angels of God ascending and descending upon the Son of Man" (John 1:51). To this skeptic, God revealed the nearness of heaven. How would Stephen see heaven? It would be when the "heavens opened," indicating that heaven was not distant but nearby, in another realm. When God opens the door to heaven, people can see into heaven. *Heaven is nearby, in another realm.*

JESUS WATCHED HEAVEN COME NEAR

At Jesus' baptism, "the heavens were opened, and he saw the Spirit of God descending as a dove, and lighting upon Him" (Matt. 3:16). When Matthew says, "The heavens were opened," he uses the normal word for opening a door (*anoigo*).[7] When a door is opened, a person sees into another realm. At the break of day, we open the front door to see the beauty of the new day—the blazing sun, the green grass, the bright red bougainvillea, and lush green trees. It is a new vista, seen from the inside of a house. In unparalleled dimension, heaven opens to a new vista, not far away, only in an entirely new—and greater and better— dimension.

Commenting on Matthew 3:16, Martin Luther said, "Heaven opens itself which hitherto was closed, and now becomes at Christ's baptism a door and a window, so that one can see into it; and hence-forth there is no difference anymore between God and us; for God the Father Himself is present and says, 'This is my beloved Son.'"[8] It is the picture of heaven drawing back its curtain to allow people to see heav-en's mysteries (cf. Job 14:12; Ps. 104:2; Isa. 40:22).[9]

Since John saw the Spirit coming down as a dove, heaven could not be far away. And the voice out of heaven was heard on earth, indicating heaven was nearby—behind the curtain—in a different sphere (Matt. 3:17). The Greek preposition *ek* ("out of") has "the strict idea 'from within,' i.e., the opened heavens."[10]

Heaven was opened to remind the people that Jesus is indeed the Son of God. The Father verified it by opening heaven and announc-ing, "This is My beloved Son, in whom I am well pleased" (Matt. 3:17). Mark is graphic in depicting the scene: "He saw the heavens opening . . ." (Mark 1:10). "Mark's use of the present tense [for "opening" (*schizom-enous*)] pictures the heavens—the sky—in the very act of being torn apart. . . . The event implies the start of a new era of open communica-tion between heaven and earth."[11] The present tense is vivid, picturing the heavens opening as something taking place in time; it is more than a mere moment.

How could the people see into heaven? How could they hear a voice, all the way from heaven (Luke 3:22)? God opened heaven by re-moving the barrier to see into another realm. He split the sky, and the people were able to look into heaven. Heaven was not far away; it was nearby!

At Jesus' transfiguration, "a bright cloud overshadowed them, and behold, a voice out of the cloud said, 'This is My beloved Son, with whom I am well-pleased; listen to Him!" (Matt. 17:5). Moses and Eli-jah, who appeared at the transfiguration, are seen as coming from God's presence in heaven, indicated further by God speaking. It is a re-minder of the nearness of heaven. Similarly, when Jesus was troubled at the impending crucifixion, "a voice came out of heaven: 'I have both glorified it, and will glorify it again'" (John 12:28). Heaven was close enough that the Father could speak to the Son to comfort Him.

When Jesus was agonizing in prayer in the garden of Gethsemane, "an angel from heaven appeared to Him, strengthening Him" (Luke 22:43). Heaven was nearby so the Father sent an angel to minister to the Son.

HEAVEN IS NEARBY

The Scriptures remind us numerous times of heaven's nearness. It is not far away; it is not in some distant universe. Scripture is replete with examples of God opening heaven for people to momentarily peer into heaven's glories. God is also heard speaking from heaven. We are limited by our physical, visual senses; yet from the Scriptures we can readily conclude that heaven is indeed not distant at all. It is nearby. *It is in another realm.*

To these Scriptures we could add numerous testimonies of believers who have been given a glorious, visual entrance into heaven, with Jesus greeting them and loved ones standing nearby, awaiting their arrival. Dear reader, you may be poring over these pages with a broken heart. A loved one has temporarily left you for heaven. Be comforted. There is a glorious reunion coming, and it is not far away. It is in another realm. Heaven is nearby—where it is *always better!* It is heaven revealed!

What is the KINGDOM CHRIST Promised?

The first recorded words of Jesus' public ministry were, "Repent, for the kingdom of heaven is at hand" (Matt. 4:17). So Christ announced the kingdom. But Jesus didn't explain the kingdom to His hearers; He assumed they understood. How could that be? His hearers were versed in the Old Testament and had heard about the coming kingdom when the Scriptures were read. They understood the nature of the kingdom that Jesus promised them.

CHRIST PROMISED AN EARTHLY KINGDOM

Christ promised a kingdom—an earthly kingdom—that would succeed the previous earthly kingdoms that culminated in the final form of the Roman kingdom (Dan. 2:40–43). The word "kingdom" denotes sovereignty, dominion, or reign. The term pictures a physical ruler who is ruling over a people living in a physical land. The word "kingdom" means "royal dominion, a designation both of the power (Ezra 4:5) and the form of government, and especially in later writers, of the territory and the rule, the kingship and the kingdom."[1] *Kingdom* then implies a king ruling over a people in a territory. The kingdom Christ spoke about relates to God's original purpose for mankind.

God's original design in creation was to fellowship with mankind in a peerless, sinless world. God created man and woman in His image and in His likeness (Gen. 1:26). Men and women have intellect, emotion, and will, and through the exercise of the heart and mind, they can engage God in fellowship. Adam and Eve enjoyed that fellowship with God for a time, but the fall destroyed the unique relationship with God.

God's original purpose in fellowship with humanity will be fulfilled in the eternal, earthly kingdom that Christ will inaugurate. That kingdom has never been abrogated, nor is it a mystical, ethereal kingdom in the heavenlies. That kingdom is the ultimate heaven—God's rule and fellowship with redeemed humanity on earth. It is the new earth that Isaiah prophesied (Isa. 65:17) and John foresaw (Rev. 21:1). Nor is there a conflict between Isaiah's words and John's vision. They are the same. It is the coming kingdom of God—heaven's rule on earth. That was God's original design in Genesis 1, and it will be fulfilled as foretold in Revelation 21.

CHRIST PROMISED AN ETERNAL KINGDOM

Earthly kingdoms do not last. Alexander the Great, the Caesars of Rome, Napoleon, the Soviet Union have all passed from the scene, as will all earthly kingdoms. This was also the message Daniel gave Nebuchadnezzar, reminding him that the kingdoms of Babylon, Medo-Persia, Greece, and Rome were temporary, but Christ's kingdom will be permanent. It will never be destroyed (Dan. 2:44); it will endure forever (Dan. 2:45). "There will be no end" to the kingdom of peace that Christ will establish (Isa. 9:7); He will rule on the throne of David forever.

The Old Testament continuously foresees an eternal, unending kingdom that Messiah will establish. God revealed to Nebuchadnezzar that Messiah's "kingdom is an everlasting kingdom and His dominion is from generation to generation" (Dan. 4:3b). Nebuchadnezzar reiterated the promise: "His dominion is an everlasting dominion, and His kingdom endures from generation to generation" (Dan. 4:34b). After Daniel spoke to Darius, the Medo-Persian king issued a decree proclaiming the God of Daniel "the living God [who endures] forever, and His kingdom is one which will not be destroyed, and His dominion will be forever" (Dan. 6:26).

In his vision prophesying the coming of Christ, Daniel exclaimed, "Behold, with the clouds of heaven one like a Son of Man was coming, and He came up to the Ancient of Days and was presented before Him. And to Him was given dominion, glory and a kingdom, that all the peoples, nations and men of every language might serve Him. His dominion is an everlasting dominion which will not pass away; and His kingdom is one which will not be destroyed" (Dan. 7:13–14). In this profound prophecy Daniel speaks of the second coming of Jesus Christ to earth to establish His kingdom. Daniel's revelation is clear: Christ's kingdom is an everlasting kingdom; it will not pass away nor be destroyed.

This is a strong statement that Christ's kingdom is eternal. These words cannot be restricted to the millennial rule of Jesus; Christ's kingdom is longer and greater than one thousand years. It is what God prepared from the beginning in Eden. It is an eternal kingdom. It is forever.

Christ's hearers understood the eternal nature of the kingdom. It would be heaven's rule on earth *forever.* Psalm 145:13 proclaims, "Your kingdom is an everlasting kingdom, and Your dominion endures throughout all generations." The kingdom Christ will establish as heaven's rule on earth will never cease, never diminish; it is eternal.

Ezekiel foresaw God's eternal kingdom alongside the conversion and restoration of the Hebrew people. He proclaimed that David[2] would be king over the Hebrew people, and they would live on the land "forever," and David would be their prince "forever" (Ezek. 37:25). At that time the Israelites will increase and worship the Lord in truth as He will set His sanctuary in their midst "forever" (Ezek. 37:26, 28). The prophet Micah also announced, "The Lord will reign over them in Mount Zion from now on and forever" (Mic. 4:7). These words cannot be restricted or limited to a thousand years.

The earthly nature of Christ's kingdom is seen in the diversity of people who will populate the kingdom. The statement, "All the peoples, nations, and men of every language might serve Him," indicates that ethnicity continues in Christ's kingdom. People from diverse cultures and languages will serve Him—Africans, Asians, Europeans, Indians, North Americans, South Americans—will continue their ethnic distinctions and worship and serve Him.

The throne that Jesus establishes will be unlike the temporal, carnal kingdoms of this world. Gabriel promised Mary that Christ "will reign over the house of Jacob forever, and His kingdom will have no end" (Luke 1:33). The use of "forever" and "have no end" are a further reminder of the eternal nature of Christ's kingdom.

These promises cannot refer only to the millennial kingdom that exists for one thousand years (Rev. 20:4–6). One thousand means one thousand; forever means forever. They are not the same. The laws of hermeneutics will not allow confining Christ's kingdom to a thousand years. The clear teaching of Scripture indicates Christ's kingdom will continue *forever*. The millennial kingdom will be a part of Christ's promised kingdom, but Christ's kingdom will continue *eternally*, beyond the millennial kingdom. Christ's kingdom will continue on the new, renovated earth (Isa. 65:17; Rev. 21:1).

CHRIST PROMISED A SPIRITUAL KINGDOM

Our world is changing rapidly, but not for the better. Same-sex marriages are being conducted in several states—and acknowledged in other countries. Couples living together without being married have become acceptable. While secularists pride themselves on this "progress," it is spiritual "regress." But a day is coming when righteousness will prevail over the entire earth. When Christ returns to inaugurate His earthly kingdom, His people will hear the wonderful words, "Come, you who are blessed of My Father, inherit the kingdom prepared for you from the foundation of the world" (Matt. 25:34).

We hear the word "inherit," and we think of something special that we receive—that someone has passed on to us. But our inheritance through Christ will surpass anything this earth has to offer. We are beneficiaries of the glorious kingdom of Christ—living on a perfect earth, enjoying, luxuriating in a perfect world, devoid of all sin. All the prophecies of Christ's glorious kingdom will culminate on the new earth, to be enjoyed by God's people.

This kingdom Christ promised will be both a physical and spiritual kingdom. Only those who are "poor in spirit" will inherit the kingdom (Matt. 5:3). Those who have been crushed in spirit (Ps. 34:18) under the weight of sin (Ps. 51:17), having seen their spiritual bankruptcy before God—these will inherit the kingdom. God Himself will dwell with those who are "contrite and lowly of spirit" (Isa. 57:15). The promise is forceful: "Theirs *is* the kingdom of heaven" (Matt. 5:3, italics added).

These are the same people who are gentle, living under God's control (Matt. 5:5). These people are "gentle, humble, considerate, meek."[3] This is dramatically different from our modern civilization and culture, which functions on the premise that those who assert themselves and gain power over others will rule. Not so. It is not the powerful, the arrogant, the self-asserting who will inherit the earth; it is those who have met the Master and King and submitted to His authority. They will rule with Him as vice regents in His kingdom.

The gentle "shall see God" (Matt. 5:8). In Christ's kingdom, on the new earth, "they will see His face" (Rev. 22:4). What a remarkable truth and awe-inspiring statement! While in the Old Testament no one could see God and live (Ex. 33:20), in Christ's kingdom believers will live in fellowship with God Himself.

CHRIST PROMISED A RESTORED EARTH

When Jesus began His public ministry, He preached, "Repent, for the kingdom of heaven is at hand" (Matt. 4:17). What was the message Jesus was proclaiming? He was offering the Hebrew people heaven's rule on earth. He was offering Israel—and through Israel the Gentile nations of the world—the restoration and renewal of all that Adam lost when he sinned in the garden of Eden.

God created Adam and Eve, commanding them to subdue and rule over the entire earth (Gen. 1:28). They were to have authority over the entire earth, living in a perfect, unstained environment. All of nature was to be in submission to the first couple. Of course, Adam's sin ruined all of that, yet numerous Scriptures point to a future day when that anticipation will indeed be fulfilled. Heaven's rule on a restored earth will be a reality. Both the Old and New Testaments point to heaven's rule on earth as the ultimate kingdom that Christ promised—the new earth, renewed and restored.

The new earth will no longer resist lush growth; the grain fields and gardens will be "rich and plenteous" (Isa. 30:23). No longer will farmers be concerned about drought or hail damaging their crops. Crop diseases will be nonexistent. On that day, when heaven joins earth, "the wilderness becomes a fertile field, and the fertile field is considered as a forest" (Isa. 32:15). The wastelands of today will be lush in abundant growth tomorrow: "The wilderness and the desert will be glad, and the Arabah will rejoice and blossom; like the crocus it will blossom profusely and rejoice with rejoicing and shout of joy" (Isa. 35:1–2a). Because the desert is pictured as productive, the metaphors depict the desert rejoicing on that day. While the imagery of joy is evident, the reality of the abundant growth remains.

CHRIST PROMISED A PEACEFUL EARTH

On August 28, 2005, Hurricane Katrina struck Louisiana, flooding 80 percent of New Orleans and causing some 1,800 deaths and $81 billion in damages. But "natural" disasters of many types occur regularly across the globe. Nature is not at peace on this present earth; hurricanes, earthquakes, and storms regularly take their toll on humanity.

Through His miracles, Christ revealed the future peaceful nature of the new earth when He establishes His kingdom. When Jesus crossed the Sea of Galilee with the disciples and a storm descended on the lake, the frightened disciples cried to Jesus for help (Luke 8:22–24). Jesus simply rebuked the wind, and the surging waves and the storm ceased (Luke 8:24; Matt. 8:26). Immediately, the sea became calm. Jesus' rebuke of the sea is significant. The word "rebuke" (*epetimesen*) "suggests that the elements are treated as evil powers which must be subdued as a sign of the kingdom over which Christ is king."[4] When Christ stilled the storm, He demonstrated His kingship over the earth, a preview of the peace on the new earth that will supplant the turmoil on the old earth.

Jesus' miracle of stilling the storm was a foretaste of Christ's rule on the new earth. Nature—everything and everyone—will be subject to Him. No more earthquakes in California, no hurricanes in Florida, no tsunamis in the Far East, no blizzards in North Dakota and the northern states, no droughts, no floods—the entire earth will be at peace, precisely the way the Lord created it to be.

But peace in Christ's kingdom will extend beyond nature; it will encompass the entire population of the earth. Wars will cease. The twentieth century and the beginnings of the twenty-first century have seen numerous wars: World Wars I and II, Korea, Vietnam, Iraq, and Afghanistan, as well as other localized wars. But Isaiah predicted a future day when "they will hammer their swords into plowshares and their spears into pruning hooks. Nation will not lift up sword against nation, and never again will they learn war" (Isa. 2:4). There will be peace among the nations of the world because Christ will be King of the earth, ruling with authority (Isa. 11:4). Christ will be installed as King in Jerusalem, governing the earth with total authority as every nation and every person submits to His authority (Ps. 2:4-9).

Zechariah sees this peace enveloping the entire earth: "I will cut off the chariot from Ephraim and the horse from Jerusalem; and the bow of war will be cut off and he will speak peace to the nations; and His dominion will be from sea to sea, and from the River to the ends of the earth" (Zech. 9:10). The comment is all encompassing; peace will prevail among the nations, and Christ's sovereign rule will cover the earth. Bible scholar Merrill Unger commented, "It does imply that there is effectiveness and authority in the word which He shall speak to bring about peace both externally and internally."[5]

Gentiles will be at peace with Israel. No longer will anyone seek the destruction of God's promised people; instead, they will come and serve the Hebrew people in farming, pasturing their flocks, and tending to their orchards (Isa. 61:5).

CHRIST PROMISED A PRODUCTIVE EARTH

God promised the prophet Ezekiel that in the coming kingdom "this desolate land will become like the garden of Eden" (Ezek. 36:35). God's original purpose for the earth will be fulfilled—it will be restored to Edenic proportions, perfect and productive. God promised,

THE KINGDOM CHRIST PROMISED

1 It is an earthly kingdom.

2 It is an eternal kingdom.

3 It is a spiritual kingdom.

4 It exists on a peaceful earth.

5 It exists on a productive earth.

6 It is a kingdom of health.

7 It is a kingdom of fellowship and celebration.

"I will multiply the fruit of the tree and the produce of the field" (Ezek. 36:30). The land will again be as highly productive as God intended for it. There will be no more "crop failures" through drought or disease. Every crop, every time, will be enormously productive.

Amos pictures the scene of agricultural productivity: "'Behold, days are coming,' declares the Lord, 'When the plowman will overtake the reaper and the treader of grapes him who sows seed; when the mountains will drip sweet wine and all the hills will be dissolved'" (Amos 9:13). Charles Feinberg described the scene this way: "The thought is that scarcely is the farmer finished plowing when the seed will be ripe, and hardly will he have completed treading the wine press when he will have to begin the sowing. (cf. Lev. 26:5). Vintage time will continue to the sowing time because of the abundance of fruit."[6] Some of the topography will change on the new earth. The desolate deserts will become productive, blossoming with beauty (Isa. 35:1–2). The endless stretch of barren desert from west of Fort Worth in Texas to Los Angeles will become lush green growth with rivers nearby. God promises, "I will even make a roadway in the wilderness, rivers in the desert" (Isa. 43:19). The animals will recognize that God has given them the abundance of water (Isa. 43:20). An abundance of trees will grow in the desert (Isa. 41:19). Together they will beautify the earth (Isa. 60:13). Land that is unproductive today will be enormously productive in Christ's kingdom.

CHRIST PROMISED A KINGDOM OF HEALTH

I watched a student walking on crutches across the seminary campus, but the following year he was confined to a wheelchair. He had multiple sclerosis, and his body continued to deteriorate. And then, just this evening, I hugged a husband and wife and wept with them. They had two adult sons: one died several years ago, and now their only remaining son died of a heart attack. We live in a world where suffering is the norm. Our bodies break down and eventually expire. But that is not what God intended for this earth.

There is a great day coming in Christ's kingdom, when all human suffering will cease. The miracles of Christ point to that glorious kingdom. Every miracle that Christ performed anticipates the coming kingdom where all maladies will be eliminated. Everyone, although living in their physical, glorified bodies, will enjoy health and youthfulness *forever*. Isaiah, prophesying about Christ's rule on earth, anticipated that great day: "Then the eyes of the blind will be opened and the ears of the deaf will be unstopped. Then the lame will leap like a deer, and the tongue of the mute will shout for joy" (Isa. 35:5–6a). When will this transpire? When the glory of the Lord envelopes the earth (Isa. 35:2).

This was the kingdom Jesus offered to the Jewish nation; if they would respond, the kingdom would be inaugurated. That was why, when Jesus healed the leper, He told him, "See that you tell no one; but go, show yourself to the priest and present the offering that Moses commanded, as a testimony to them" (Matt. 8:4). The healing was a witness to the Jewish leaders—and a provocation for them to recognize the Messiah. Had they recognized Him, the eternal kingdom of Christ would have been inaugurated.

Illnesses that ravage the body will be nonexistent in Christ's kingdom. Christ healed many sick people with diverse illnesses: He healed a woman with a hemorrhage (Matt. 9:20–22), one man possessed by demons (Matt. 9:32–34; Matt. 12:22), another with a withered hand (Matt. 12:9–14), an epileptic boy (Matt. 17:14–18), Peter's mother-in-law (Luke 4:38–39), and those with numerous other diseases (Luke 4:40–41). And not nearly all the miracles Christ performed are recorded. John reminds us, "Therefore many other signs Jesus also performed in the presence of the disciples, which are not written in this book; but these have been written so that you may believe that Jesus is the Christ, the Son of God; and that believing you may have life in His name" (John 20:30–31). The sign (*semeiov*) was "an act or miracle with a meaning designed to lead to belief in Jesus as the Messiah, the Son of God."[7] Each sign pointed to Jesus and to the kingdom He would one day inaugurate.

Of particular significance was Jesus' healing of the blind. There are more recorded miracles of Jesus healing the blind than those with any other illness—and there were spiritual overtones. When Jesus healed the blind men at Jericho (Matt. 20:29–34), it was a reminder that there will be no physical blindness in Messiah's kingdom. But it also revealed that there will be *no spiritual blindness* in the kingdom—not by God's chosen people nor by the Gentiles. All will have knowledge of Christ, and all will worship Him.

The climactic message in Christ's miracles is that death is defeated and destroyed forever. Standing near the grave of His friend Lazarus, Jesus promised Martha, "I am the resurrection and the life; he who believes in Me will live even if he dies, and everyone who lives and believes in Me will never die" (John 11:25–26). Jesus came to give life, *eternal, unending life*—and that would be the joy, the undergirding of the kingdom. No death! When Jesus came to Lazarus' tomb, He cried out with a loud voice, "Lazarus, come forth" (John 11:43) and Lazarus got up and walked out. This was a vivid picture of life in the kingdom—no more death. Christ has forever abolished death, rendering Satan powerless (Heb. 2:14–15). In the kingdom there will be continuing, ongoing, unending life—both qualitative and quantitative. Rejoice in the anticipation!

CHRIST PROMISED A KINGDOM OF
FELLOWSHIP AND CELEBRATION

What was the significance of the miracle when Jesus changed the water into wine at Cana (John 2:1–11)? Having tasted the wine that Jesus had produced, the headwaiter exclaimed, "You have kept the good wine until now" (John 2:10). It was a reminder of the *quality* that Jesus produced. It was a wedding, a time of celebration. Now Jesus provided wine of unusual quality, pointing to the kingdom when good quality will be the norm. Everything will be better.

But there is more. Just as the wedding was a time of celebration, Jesus' miracle is a reminder of the qualitative celebration we will enjoy in heaven. Endless rapture. We will be so fulfilled in fellowship and celebration with family and friends and the Lord Jesus that there is no old earthly experience to compare. The present fellowship we enjoy is only a foretaste of the joy in Christ's kingdom (John 15:11; 16:24).

The feeding of the multitudes (Matt. 14:13–21; Mark 6:33–44; Luke 9:12–17; John 6:5–13) pointed to the time of fellowship and celebration in Christ's kingdom. When the multitudes came to hear Christ, He had them recline in groups of about fifty each while he kept giving the disciples the loaves and fish to feed the people. What was the result? "They all ate and were satisfied" (Luke 9:17). "Satisfied" (*echortasthesan*) is graphic; it is used for animals that gorge themselves. It means they have eaten to their fill.[8] The miracle is a strong picture of the fellowship that will ultimately be ours in Christ's kingdom.

Isaiah pictured the banquet scene in Messiah's kingdom: "The Lord of hosts will prepare a lavish banquet for all peoples on this mountain; a banquet of aged wine, choice pieces with marrow, and refined, aged wine" (Isa. 25:6). The banquet Isaiah describes overflows with choice food and good fellowship.

Jesus Himself described the kingdom as "compared to a king who gave a wedding feast for his son" (Matt. 22:2). What would a wedding feast arranged by a king for his son be like? Lavish! Imagine heaven's rule on earth in Christ's kingdom, pictured as a king's wedding banquet for his son—and that is precisely what the kingdom will be. The church is the bride of Christ. The kingdom will be the eternal celebration of the wedding of Christ and the church. We will enjoy rapturous celebration as the bride of Christ in the eternal kingdom.

With whom will we fellowship? With family and friends and Christ! Jesus promised, "Many will come from east and west, and recline at the table with Abraham, Isaac and Jacob in the kingdom of heaven" (Matt. 8:11). Who are Abraham, Isaac, and Jacob? Grandfather, father, and son. It is a family fellowship. That is the glory of Christ's kingdom that we can anticipate with joy and excitement. Reunion with our believing loved ones and friends, together in fellowship with Christ Himself. What a phenomenal prospect! Celebration and fulfilling fellowship with loved ones—ongoing, unending in Christ's kingdom. What could be greater?

Can you begin to imagine, to fathom the glory, the wonder, the excitement, the joy that will be ours living and celebrating in Christ's kingdom? Keep focused. Amid the sorrow and suffering in this troubled world, keep focused. "Seek first His kingdom" (Matt. 6:33). "Blessed are you who weep now, for you shall laugh" (Luke 6:21). You will be in the kingdom where it is *always better—in every way*. It is heaven revealed!

What Kind of BODY

Will We HAVE?

Our society places great emphasis and value on a beautiful human body. As a young man I was involved in boxing and followed the famous prizefighters. Sugar Ray Robinson had the unique distinction of holding the lightweight, welterweight, and middleweight world championships. He had a powerful, muscular body and was deemed the best prize-fighter, "pound for pound"—a unique distinction.

Magazine and newspaper ads display beautiful women modeling clothing. Billboards and showrooms feature the latest styles in men's and women's fashions. Everywhere we look, the emphasis is on the outward body: manicured nails, hair salons, gyms to slim the body, liposuction to remove unsightly, sagging skin.

But these earthly bodies are temporal. Sugar Ray Robinson did not remain strong and muscular. The beautiful women who parade the pages of the papers become old and wrinkled. These bodies don't remain young and beautiful. And these bodies will not enter heaven in their present state.

The Scripture says, "Flesh and blood cannot inherit the kingdom of God" (1 Cor. 15:50). This is a serious, provocative statement that raises the question, "What kind of body will we have in the resurrection?" Artists who try to imagine resurrected bodies are notoriously deficient in biblical knowledge, but we are not left in darkness and confusion concerning our resurrection body. The Scriptures are quite clear—and the following biblical truths concerning our resurrection body should provide us enormous comfort and cause us to rejoice and praise God for His goodness to us.

WE WILL HAVE AN INTERMEDIATE BODY

The resurrection body that the Scripture describes is the new body we will receive at the resurrection (1 Cor. 15:51–53). But what happens at death, before the resurrection? Recall that at the transfiguration of Christ, Moses and Elijah appeared to James, Peter, and John (Matt. 17:3). The three disciples recognized Moses and Elijah. Clearly, those two had physical bodies through which they were identifiable. Peter immediately recognized them in their physical form (Matt. 17:4). They are identified as "men" (Luke 9:30), hardly the designation of a spirit.

In heaven, prior to the resurrection, the elders are seen falling down and casting their crowns before the throne (Rev. 4:10), all of which necessitates a physical body. They are also seen holding harps and golden bowls (Rev. 5:8).

The conclusion? Though we don't know all the specifics of a believer's resurrection body, "at death [we will not be] bodiless or disembodied[;] there is provided a body from heaven which may serve the believer until the resurrection, when he receives his body from the grave."[1] Thus those who die before the resurrection of the dead will have intermediate bodies before they receive their final bodies during the resurrection.

OUR FINAL BODY WILL BE LIKE CHRIST'S

Upon Jesus' return, however, we receive a body like Christ's resurrection body. First John 3:2 tells us, "Beloved, now we are children of God, and it has not appeared as yet what we will be. We know that when He appears, we will be like Him, because we will see Him just as He is." The phrase, "We will be like Him," is an astounding promise. We shall be like Christ, and we shall reflect His glory. B. F. Westcott explains, "This likeness of man redeemed and perfected to God is the likeness of the creature reflecting the glory of the Creator."[2] All of creation is designed to glorify the greatness of the Creator. The ultimate reflection of the Creator's glory will be the redemption and glorification of our body, when at the rapture, our bodies are transformed into the image of Christ (1 Thess. 4:16–17; 1 Cor. 15:51–56).

On that momentous day we will instantaneously "be changed" (1 Cor. 15:51). "Changed" is used for a hyena changing its nature and for stones changing their color.[3] The hyena remains a hyena—but it has a radically new nature; its ferocity is gone. The stone remains a stone, but it has a new, vibrant color. "Changed" means "changed into something far better and vastly superior to the former"—yet there remains the identity and continuity with the old. We remain the same persons, yet we are renovated into perfection in every respect.

Jesus Christ came so that many would follow in His path—that was God's eternal purpose for humanity: "For those whom He foreknew, He also predestined to become conformed to the image of His Son, so that He might be the firstborn among many brethren; and these whom He predestined, He also called, and these whom He called, He also justified, and these whom He justified, He also glorified" (Rom. 8:29–30). Christ was "the firstborn among many brethren," meaning many would receive glorified bodies as well. And God will fulfill that promise for believers when He glorifies them on that future day. As we have borne the image of the earthly body from Adam, so we will bear the image of the heavenly, spiritual body from Christ (1 Cor. 15:49).

WE WILL HAVE A REAL BODY
AND A FAMILIAR VOICE

We will have a real body with a real voice—and we will recognize each other's voice. For most of our married years, I called Helen, "Heln." I would omit the last "e." The last few years Helen reminded me that her name was spelled H-e-l-e-n, so I learned to carefully pronounce her name "Hel*en*." She, on the other hand, affectionately called me "Ennsie." That was her endearing term for me. No one else called me Ennsie; that was for Helen alone. I will rejoice when I enter glory and hear her call, "Ennsie!" What joy we will have when we hear our loved ones call our name!

Mary was in the garden, grieving over the death of Jesus, but when He called, "Mary!" she immediately recognized both Him and His voice (John 20:16). Jesus' resurrection body carried the same intonation in His voice that reminded Mary of the bygone days of fellowship with Christ. She also recognized Him in His physical form and wanted to cling to Him (John 20:17). It was the same Jesus in voice and body—except now He had a glorified body.

Following the resurrection, Jesus appeared to the Twelve, showing them the nail marks in His hands and the wound in His side (John 20:20). Jesus invited the doubting Thomas to touch His hands and His side—verifiable proof that He was the same corporeal Jesus who had been crucified days earlier (John 20:27). Still later Jesus met the weary disciples at the Sea of Galilee. He cooked them a breakfast of bread and fish and ate with them—proof of a genuinely physical body (John 21:1–14).

WE WILL HAVE A RECOGNIZABLE BODY

Uppermost in most people's minds is the question, "Will I recognize my husband, my wife, my parents, my son, my daughter in heaven?"

OUR PERFECT BODY IN HEAVEN

1. Before the resurrection, we will have an intermediate body.

2. Our final body will be like Christ's.

3. We will have a real body and a familiar voice.

4. We will have a recognizable body.

5. We will have an imperishable body.

6. We will have a glorified body.

7. We will have a powerful body.

8. We will have a spiritual body.

9. Our body will have no limitations.

This question tears at the heart of people. The ones we loved on earth are important to us! Helen was constantly smiling—I will want to see her smiling face. I will want to see my brother, with his relaxed outward gait when he walked. I will want to see my sons and their families, my parents . . . friends . . . these are important and deep desires.

Will we recognize our loved ones? Yes! Scripture is abundantly clear on the issue. Jesus showed Himself to numerous people following His resurrection. Mary saw Him and recognized Him and ran and told the disciples that she had seen Him (John 20:18). The Twelve saw Him and heard Him speak and recognized it was Jesus (Matt. 28:9). He showed the disciples His wounds, and they rejoiced as they saw Him, recognizing it was the same Jesus (John 20:20). They impressed on Thomas that they had seen Him (John 20:25). They concluded it was the same Jesus who had risen from the dead. Jesus appeared to Thomas, showing him His wounds and admonishing him for not believing He had been raised from the dead. It was the recognizable Jesus whom they knew and loved. It was He!

The appearances of Jesus are a reminder that the resurrection body carries a continuity with the former earthly body. It is also a reminder that we will recognize one another in our particular voice as well as our body. We will be identifiable as the same person we were on earth, but with a new, glorified, indestructible body.

WE WILL HAVE AN IMPERISHABLE BODY

I was shocked as I reviewed my father's family record. His mother had recorded the ages of my father's siblings at death: Jacob, ten; Peter, thirty-one; David, nineteen; Johan, one; Anna, one; Anna II, two; Jacob II, twenty-four; Isaak, zero (he died in his first year); my father, Isaak II, forty-eight. Another sister, Aganeta, died as a young mother. Among his nine siblings, my father lived the longest, and he died at forty-eight. The average lifespan may be much longer today, but we all still have perishable bodies. Yet the Bible promises a great day is coming when "this perishable [will] put on the imperishable" (1 Cor. 15:53). Think of it! You will have a body that will *never perish*. Nor will it face debilitating diseases. Every believer will have a youthful body—forever.

Our physical body, now subject to sin, decay, and death, will be indestructible in heaven and no longer subject to control by sin.

No sickness or aging. Get the picture? Black and brown hair will not turn gray with age; skin won't become flabby and sag; teeth won't rot. There will be no headaches, stomachaches, diabetes, cancer, or heart ailments. The maladies will belong to the former life; they belong to the old world. On the new earth—heaven—we each will have a perfect body, resistant to any ailment. Our new body will continue on forever, without missing a beat.

Joni Eareckson Tada, a paraplegic since age seventeen, says she is looking forward to a new nature, with pure motives. It is an interesting statement from one who is also looking forward to a new body to replace the one immobilized in a diving accident. Yes, on that day we will have a new body *and* a new mind.

WE WILL HAVE A GLORIFIED BODY

Our present body "is sown in dishonor" (1 Cor. 15:43) as the body is placed in the grave to decay. "Dishonor" means "humiliation"[4] and is "used of loss of rights of citizenship. A corpse has no rights."[5] It pictures the body going into the grave. But that is not the end of the story.

My grandson, Jacob, planted a watermelon seed, and several months later he lifted a large, luscious, red watermelon. He also planted a banana tree and later (with the help of his father) picked a stalk of over one hundred fifty bananas. All of nature is a reminder of the coming glory of the resurrection. From a tiny seed, new life is born.

At the resurrection, the body that has been subject to decay is raised in glory (1 Cor. 15:43). The Lord Jesus Christ "will transform the body of our humble state into conformity with the body of His glory, by the exerting of the power that He has even to subject all things to Himself" (Phil. 3:21). Christ will transform (*metaschematisei*)—"refashion . . . change the outward form or appearance" of—these tired bodies into the conformity, the "changing of the inward and outward substance"[6] of our body like the glorious body of Christ.

"Glory" suggests the resurrection body will exhibit "that resplendent brightness which diffuses light and awakens admiration. It is to be fashioned like unto the glorious body of the Son of God."[7] Our resurrection bodies will be "radiant with the brightness of perfect life."[8]

It is a reminder that our bodies will be incomparable in beauty. If we reflect on our early days of adulthood, how we met our spouses, undoubtedly, there was physical attraction, an attraction of beauty. I clearly recall the first good look I got at Helen. When I saw her, I was smitten. I immediately said to myself, "That's the woman I'm going to marry!" I was overcome by her beauty, her cheerful smile, and her sparkling, brown eyes. When we see one another in heaven, we will have beautiful bodies that will far surpass the beauty of our bodies on this earth.

WE WILL HAVE A POWERFUL BODY

In their prime, athletes perform with brilliance. I recall the day I heard that Roger Bannister broke four minutes in running one mile. It was a magnificent feat—and many since then have pared the time down to run the mile even faster. But it is not long before the athlete can no longer run a four-minute mile—and there comes a day when he may not be able to *walk* a mile. Our bodies continue to deteriorate. In my hospital visits I see the sad deterioration of the body until finally it gives up. Death occurs.

But the resurrection body will be a body of power (1 Cor. 15:43). "There is no indication that it will need sleep or food."[9]

Beyond escaping sickness and disease, our powerful body will never again face physical, emotional, or mental pain. No emotional upset will ever disturb the resurrection body, no limited thinking. As I get older, I realize the "files" in the mind become more difficult to find! Loss of memory increases with age. As a good friend of mine, when he can't remember a name or an item, says, "Let me get back to you on that!" There will be no limitations of any kind in our new body of power.

Unquestionably, our resurrection body will be endowed "with faculties of which we have now no conception."[10] We will have strength, energy, abilities, and use of all faculties in an inconceivable dimension. We will think thoughts never before realized; we will see, hear, smell, and taste in a profoundly greater way. Our body will be tireless. Never again will we say or hear someone say, "Oh, I'm so tired!"

WE WILL HAVE A SPIRITUAL BODY

The body of this earth is a natural body; it has limitations, especially spiritual limitations. The new body will be a spiritual body (1 Cor. 15:44). Yet it will also be a fully physical body. Jesus' resurrection body had all the faculties of a material body. There was a physical continuity with His former body, demonstrated in the nail prints in His hands and wound in His side. Further, Jesus talked, ate, and functioned in a normal physical way. But the resurrection body will be heightened spiritually. "In the material body the spirit has been limited and hampered in its action; in the future body it will have perfect freedom of action and consequently complete control, and man will at last be, what God created him to be, a being in which the higher self is supreme."[11] "Spiritual" emphasizes the medium through which the believer has communion with God. In the resurrection body, the spiritual is developed "according to a higher law which is quite beyond our comprehension."[12]

In this life we are exhorted to "walk by the Spirit," to be controlled by the Holy Spirit (Gal. 5:16). In that future day when we each receive a resurrection body, we walk according to the Spirit the way God intended for us to walk—it will then be our *normal life.* The prohibitions of the epistles will be unnecessary. There will be no jealousy, strife, or anger, no unkind word, no drunkenness or immorality. No one will ever again say, "I wish I hadn't said that."

As a normal condition of our new resurrection body, we will exhibit love, joy, peace, patience, kindness, goodness, faithfulness, gentleness, and self-control. They will be the natural and normal function of our new body.

OUR BODY WILL HAVE NO LIMITATIONS

God will "transform the body of our humble state into conformity with the body of His glory" (Phil. 3:21). What kind of a body did Christ have? We have already noted that He had a physical body that exhibited continuity with His earthly body. But it was also a body of glory, without physical limitations. Although the doors were shut and locked, Jesus suddenly appeared to the disciples (John 20:19, 26). While He had a physical body of flesh and bones (Luke 24:39), He could pass through doors unhindered. He could appear and disappear at will (Luke 24:31, 36).

Similarly, our resurrection body will not be less physical, but they shall also be without physical and spiritual limitations. Physically, we will be identifiable according to our earthly appearance, yet without physical limitations. We will possess a body of glory, like the glorious body of Jesus Christ. Spiritually, we will be dominated only by our re-generated spirit; we will no longer possess the old nature with the old mind, old heart, and old will. What a phenomenally wonderful day that will be! It is heaven—*always better.* It is heaven revealed!

What is the RELATIONSHIP of the Millennium to HEAVEN?

While attending the Christian Booksellers Association Convention in Denver one year, I stayed at the downtown Hyatt Hotel. One evening I rode an elevator to the 27th floor, took a seat in a comfortable chair, and began to gaze out the panoramic windows facing the west.

I didn't eat, drink, or read. For an hour I just sat there, entranced as I gazed westward. I was awestruck at God's marvelous creation of the majestic mountains and the brilliance of the sun setting over the Rocky Mountains. I was fixated on the breathtaking beauty of God's creation, and I responded with praise and prayer to God.

The Lord has created a beautiful earth, a majestic earth. When Jesus rules during the millennium, this earth will be even more breathtaking. But an important question arises: What is the relationship of this beautiful earth to the eternal state? Will this beautiful earth endure only in the millennium?

We can discover some wonderful truths about the eternal state—

heaven—in the Old Testament. Parallel passages that seem to refer to the millennium in the Old Testament are seen to refer to the eternal state in the New Testament. This challenges our thinking and our understanding of heaven.

THERE IS CONTINUITY FROM THE
MILLENNIAL KINGDOM TO THE ETERNAL STATE

The book of Revelation is chronological in its format: Chapters 1 to 3 deal with the churches of the first century; chapters 4 to 19 discuss the future tribulation period; chapter 19 discusses the second coming of Christ; and chapter 20 discusses the millennial kingdom and the great white throne judgment at the end of the millennium.

The final two chapters, 21 and 22, detail the eternal state. In describing the eternal state, the apostle John begins, "Then I saw a new heaven and a new earth; for the first heaven and the first earth passed away, and there is no longer any sea" (Rev. 21:1). But Isaiah mentions the same phrase: "For behold, I create new heavens and a new earth" (Isa. 65:17). Later Isaiah discusses what is normally understood as a millennial passage (when Messiah rules one thousand years). He talks of building houses, of planting vineyards, of the wolf grazing with the lamb, and the lion eating straw like an ox (Isa. 65:20–25). Admittedly, he refers to infants and old men, of a youth dying at the age of one hundred. There is no discussion of whether that is millennial or not. It is. There will be no aging or death in heaven in the eternal state.

However, the question remains: Since Isaiah and John use the same phrase, and John uses it for the eternal state, could Isaiah 65 reflect a continuity between the millennial kingdom and the eternal state? I think it does. Many other passages will confirm this thesis.

Bible scholar Herbert M. Wolf agrees with this premise. "The description of the messianic age in [Isaiah 65] verses 17–25 in many respects could find its fulfillment during the Millennium, but some of the features of Isaiah's description of the messianic age seem to look ahead to the eternal state."[1] As Wolf considers the new heaven and the new earth, he concludes, "It is somewhat artificial to distinguish the new heaven and new earth from . . . the rule of Messiah [the millennial kingdom]. Isaiah understood all of them as the culmination of God's work of salvation, and it is difficult to divide them into separate categories."[2] He concludes that there are parallel passages that deal with both the millennial kingdom and the new heaven and the new earth.

Erwin Lutzer concludes, "It is reasonable to assume that there is continuity between the earthly kingdom and the eternal heavenly kingdom."[3] And that continuity is evident through the many phrases that refer to passages normally assigned to the millennial kingdom, while, without dispute, the same phrases describe the heavenly eternal state. The conclusion must be that many of the passages that describe the millennial kingdom also, in continuity, describe the new heaven and the new earth—the eternal state.

Herman Hoyt, former president of Grace College and Grace Theological Seminary, draws a similar conclusion: "Quite evidently the text carries the notion of saved peoples in the new earth living as Adam lived before the fall. This has led some to remand this passage to the millennium. But other men are firmly convinced that this speaks of the eternal state, and that these peoples are living in the natural state that God originally intended for Adam and his race."[4]

Clearly, there is a continuity of this present earth into the millennium, but beyond that, into the eternal state. The earth will continue forever, though as a new, renovated earth. "The new world will not be without [connection] with the old world. The coming earth is not 'another' but a 'new' one. Otherwise it could not be called a 'new *earth.*' No, if John sees a new 'heaven' and a new 'earth,' this proves that even in eternity the distinction between our planet and the heavenly places will in some fashion continue."[5]

CHRIST'S KINGDOM WILL ENDURE FOREVER

God said, "I create new heavens and a new earth" (Isa. 65:17). While this is frequently delegated to the millennium, a valid question is this: "Does God create a new heavens and a new earth only for one thousand years?" Undoubtedly not. And this is verified by John's similar statement describing the eternal state (Rev. 21:1). The new heavens and the new earth are eternal.

The Scriptures consistently emphasize that the kingdom that Christ establishes will endure forever. It will never be terminated. Isaiah says, "There will be no end to the increase of His government or of peace, on the throne of David and over his kingdom, to establish it and to uphold it with justice and righteousness from then on and forevermore" (Isa. 9:7). The words "no end" and "forevermore" are comprehensive. They say what they mean—they cannot be restricted to one thousand years. Christ's kingdom will endure forever. Isaiah specifies that the cypress and myrtle trees will prevail "forever" in Messiah's kingdom (Isa. 55:13).

The covenant that God has made with Israel will prevail forever; they will enjoy Messiah's blessing forever (Isa. 59:21). Israel will possess the promised land "forever" (Isa. 60:21). Because of their position in God's plan, Israel will have "everlasting joy" (Isa. 61:7). In that day, God's glory will illuminate the new earth as "an everlasting light," never to be snuffed out (Isa. 60:19).

Merrill Unger sees a continuity of the millennial kingdom into eternity. He states:

> Isaiah's vision, while glimpsing the Kingdom age, the last ordered age in time, is projected into eternity. He saw the Millennium merging into the final state of bliss and having an everlasting feature to it, according to the Davidic Covenant (2 Sam. 7:13, 16). So the prophecy employs language that, although applicable to a degree to millennial conditions, will be

fully realized on the regenerated earth . . . they blend in Isaiah's vision with eternal conditions, of which they are a thrilling harbinger.[6]

In the Davidic covenant, God promised David that his descendant —the Messiah—would inaugurate a kingdom that would endure "forever," and His throne "shall be established forever" (2 Sam. 7:16). Psalm 89 speaks similarly: "I have made a covenant with My chosen; I have sworn to David My servant, I will establish your seed forever, and build up your throne to all generations" (Ps. 89:3–4).

These passages are frequently understood to refer to the millennium, and that is undoubtedly true, but when the term "forever" is used, it cannot be limited to the thousand years of the millennium. Clearly, there is a sense of continuity with the eternal state.

DANIEL AND JOHN
DECLARE AN ETERNAL KINGDOM

What kind of a kingdom is the Scripture discussing? Some would suggest it is a heavenly kingdom in a mystical sense. Some say it is fulfilled in the present church age. The Scriptures give strong evidence that the kingdom will be an earthly kingdom that begins in the future age when Messiah returns to rule in a perfect world on the new earth.

The prophet Daniel says, "In the days of those kings the God of heaven will set up a kingdom which will never be destroyed . . . it will itself endure forever" (Dan. 2:44). Daniel has previously discussed the earthly kingdoms of Babylon, Medo-Persia, Greece, and Rome (vv. 36–43). What were these kingdoms? They were *earthly* kingdoms. Daniel explains that "in the days of those kings" Christ will establish His kingdom. Clearly, it will be an earthly kingdom. But this kingdom, while inaugurating the millennium, will extend beyond the millennium because Daniel says this kingdom will "never be destroyed"; it will "endure forever."

Daniel's declaration that Christ's kingdom will "endure forever" indicates it continues beyond the millennium into eternity. Christ's kingdom and the conditions of the millennium will reflect the conditions on the new earth for eternity.

Daniel describes the Son of Man returning to establish the kingdom and promises, "His dominion is an everlasting dominion which will not pass away; and His kingdom is one which will not be destroyed" (Dan. 7:14). In this prophetic vision Daniel is also told that "His kingdom will be an everlasting kingdom" (Dan. 7:27). The promise is clear. Messiah's kingdom is "everlasting"; it "will not pass away," and "will not be destroyed." There is no other way to understand this except that it is a permanent, everlasting, and eternal kingdom.

In Scripture's final book, Revelation, John also says, "The kingdom of the world has become the kingdom of our Lord and of His Christ; and He will reign forever and ever" (Rev. 11:15). These words confirm that it is both an earthly kingdom and an eternal kingdom. The earthly kingdom will endure throughout eternity.

An Eternal Eden Will Reappear

Since Isaiah (Isa. 65:17) and John (Rev. 21:1) both describe the new heaven and the new earth, it is reasonable to conclude that many of the conditions Isaiah describes in chapter 65 refer not only to the millennium, but also to the eternal state on the new earth. God's original purpose also demands this.

What was God's original purpose in creation? God created man for fellowship. He came down to Eden to fellowship with mankind (Gen. 3:8). The fall of man ruined that, and Paradise—that is, the garden of Eden—was lost, but on the new earth, paradise will be regained and God will again fellowship with mankind in a unique sense on the new earth. That is particularly the point of the New Jerusalem coming down out of heaven (Rev. 21:2). God's original plan of fellowship with man on earth will indeed culminate on the new earth.

THE MILLENNIUM AND HEAVEN

1 There is continuity from the millennial kingdom to the eternal state.

2 Christ's kingdom will endure forever.

3 The prophet Daniel and the apostle John declare an ongoing, eternal kingdom.

4 An eternal Eden will reappear.

5 The people of Israel will return to the land and live there forever.

6 Gentiles and Jews will forever worship the King.

The new earth will have Eden everywhere, as earth is restored to Eden-like conditions with peace in every realm—in the animal world and in the plant world. People will build homes on the new earth without worrying about floods, hurricanes, or earthquakes. They will reap bumper crops in their harvesting—no drought, blight, flood, or infestation will ruin their crops (Isa. 65:21b; Amos 9:13; Ezek. 34:26–27).

Isaiah 11 is similar in thought to Isaiah 65, and while it refers to the millennial kingdom, it undoubtedly also refers to life on the new earth in the eternal state. There will be peace in the animal world (Isa. 11:5–9); animals will be submissive and will no longer harm people (Ezek. 34:25). It is the time when Christ rules as king over the Hebrew people and over the entire world (Ezek. 34:23–24). Christ's reign of peace will continue forever on the new earth: "There will be no end to the increase of His government or of peace [it will continue] from then on and forevermore" (Isa. 9:7). The picture of peace in Isaiah 11:6–9 takes the reader back to the garden of Eden, where wild animals will not kill. It is an eternal time of entire peace and safety on the New Earth.

ISRAEL WILL RETURN TO THE LAND
AND LIVE THERE FOREVER

The Hebrew people are God's chosen people, and their election is not restricted to time. God made an everlasting covenant with them (Isa. 55:3; 61:8). Their existence will continue forever; David's throne will continue through all generations—it will endure forever (Ps. 89:4; Isa. 9:7). When the nation is converted, the Hebrew people will experience "everlasting joy" (Isa. 61:7).

During the tribulation there will be a national turning of Israel to the Lord; they will walk in righteousness (Rom. 11:26-27). When Israel is restored during the tribulation and established in the land, God promises that they will live on the land that He gave to Jacob for all generations, "forever," and David will be their king "forever" (Ezek. 37:25). God established an everlasting covenant with Israel, and it will be of everlasting duration. God Himself will be in their midst "forever" (Ezek. 37:26).

GENTILES AND JEWS WILL
FOREVER WORSHIP THE KING

Hebrew people will come from distant lands, summoned to worship at the capital city of the world: Jerusalem. Those who had been oppressed and suffered in foreign lands will come. They will be converted and will converge on Jerusalem to worship Jesus Christ as their Lord and Messiah (Isa. 27:13). While this glorious event occurs at the beginning of the millennium, it continues into the eternal kingdom. Isaiah also prophesies a future day when all mankind will come to Jerusalem, bow down to the Lord, and worship (Isa. 66:23). The prophet sees the future day of the new heavens and the new earth, the eternal state, when this will take place.

Zechariah also describes that day when Gentiles will come and worship the Lord in Jerusalem in the millennium (Zech. 14:16). This worship culminates the judgment of the nations at the inauguration of the millennial kingdom (Zech. 14:12f.). In that future day all groups will be gathered to worship the Lord in the eternal state (Heb. 12:22).

The glories of the kingdom that Christ will establish at His second coming will persist throughout the millennium and continue for all eternity on the new earth. Scripture provides abundant support that there is a continuity between the millennium and the eternal state on the new earth. It will be glorious. It will be heaven revealed!

What and When Are the NEW HEAVEN and the NEW EARTH?

Who has not seen the breathtaking scenery of the Austrian countryside in *The Sound of Music*, with Julie Andrews sweeping across the hills in joyful song? Austria indeed is a beautiful country.

I'm partial to Austria, it being my homeland. My wife and I traveled throughout Austria nearly a dozen times. We enjoyed sitting on the balcony of our favorite bed and breakfast at Mondsee, seeing the lake below and the mountains in the distance. The scenery in Portschach, "the Austrian Riviera," is similarly beautiful. Traveling through the spectacular mountains and valleys, the mountain roads southeast of Innsbruck were vivid reminders of our great Creator God.

Of course, the beauty of this earth is not limited to Austria. God's creative beauty is evident on all seven continents, from the dazzling glaciers of Antarctica to the rugged mountains of the Andes in South America to the Rockies in North America.

This raises some pertinent questions. What is the future of God's magnificent creation? Will this earth be totally destroyed? What is the new earth? Does it have any relationship to the present earth? While we look forward to a new heaven, let's first consider the new earth, for the new earth will indeed be like heaven on earth.

WE WILL BEHOLD A NEW EARTH

We will live on a restored earth. The new heaven helps define the new earth. The new earth will not be some ethereal entity, but is depicted in Scripture as being an "earth," with all the components that we understand as "earth." While John writes from an eternal perspective in the chronology of Revelation in describing the new heaven and the new earth (Rev. 21:1), Isaiah gives specifics concerning the new heaven and the new earth (Isa. 65:17ff.).[1] Isaiah sees people building homes and inhabiting them, planting vineyards, and eating the fruit (Isa. 65:21). He sees peace in the animal kingdom (Isa. 65:25). God's glory will radiate through the world, with the Gentile people recognizing the Lord as God, and they will come and worship in Jerusalem (Isa. 66:18–20).

Christ will rule from Jerusalem, exalted upon the earth, and everyone will recognize His rule and submit to it (Phil. 2:11).

God created humanity so He could have fellowship with man and woman. God came down to the garden of Eden for fellowship with mankind—and God's original purpose will be fulfilled on the new earth. The old earth will be restored to a new earth where man will be fulfilled in "various kinds of meaningful activity, learning and serving the Lord."[2]

We will live on a productive land. On the new earth the land will prosper without the effects of sin. The land will yield an abundant harvest, unlike anything on this sin-laden earth. There will be no resistance to the growth of crops. Isaiah promises, "The wilderness becomes a fertile field, and the fertile field is considered as a forest" (Isa. 32:15). Amid the perfected, renewed earth will be justice and righteousness (Isa. 32:16). Through Amos God paints a similar picture of prosperity: "'The plowman will overtake the reaper and the treader of grapes him who sows seed" (Amos 9:13). The harvest will be so enormous, the one who begins to plant seeds for another harvest will overtake the harvester.

We will live on a peaceful earth. Driving along the Rhine River valley in Germany, seeing the hillsides covered with grapes, one can only imagine the future day when the hillsides will be still richer in a phenomenal harvest of grapes. But isn't this a picture of the millennium? No, it reaches far beyond the millennium. Isaiah reminds us that amid the restoration of nature in all its magnificence and beauty, will be peace and quietness "forever" (Isa. 32:17). What a glorious hope; what a wonderful promise.

Our world is not a peaceful world. In nature we experience the ravages of hurricanes, earthquakes, blizzards, floods, and droughts. And on the human level, there is political turmoil, terrorism, and crime. But we can look forward expectantly to a beautified, restored earth where there is complete peace, tranquility, and safety. No crime. No storms. Only peace. What a hope!

THREE ELEMENTS MARK A RESTORED EARTH

There is continuity. Peter prophesied a cataclysmic event for the present earth: "But the day of the Lord will come like a thief, in which the heavens will pass away with a roar and the elements will be destroyed with intense heat, and the earth and its works will be burned up" (2 Pet. 3:10). What was Peter referring to? Was he describing the total destruction of this earth? Actually, no. Peter was describing the renovation of the old earth. Later he says, "We are looking for new heavens and a new earth, in which righteousness dwells" (2 Pet. 3:13). While it is "new," it is still "earth." The term "earth" is a reminder of the continuity of the new earth with the old earth. But it will be a newly renovated earth—cleansed by fire "into a perfect earth where the redeemed will live for all eternity. . . . out of the ashes of the old earth will be made the new one."[3]

The "new earth" does not imply "a cosmos totally other than the present one" but a renewed earth, "in continuity with the present one."[4]

God's original purpose will be fulfilled. Will the earth be destroyed? While that is the conclusion of some, it cannot be so for several reasons. When God created the earth, He made it for mankind. Man was destined to rule as king of the earth, in a perfect environment.[5] When God had completed His creation, He called it "very good" (Gen. 1:31). God did not create the earth very good only to have Satan lead man in rebellion against God, causing God to destroy the world. Were that the case, Satan could claim a victory. "It is difficult to think that God would entirely annihilate his original creation, thereby seeming to give the devil the last word and scrapping the creation that was originally 'very good' (Gen. 1:31)," writes theologian Wayne Grudem.[6]

Thus a restored earth is part of fulfilling God's original purpose. Erich Sauer is correct when he says, "God will not annihilate but 'change' (Psa. 102:26), not reject but redeem, not destroy but set in order, not abolish but create anew, not ruin but transfigure."[7]

While the earth is called "new," "this does not mean 'new' in the absolute sense; for 'the earth abides forever' (Eccl. 1:4; cf. Ps. 104:5; 119:90). Neither heaven or earth will be annihilated."[8] Further, the term "passing away" ("*parerchomai*") has a wide range of meanings. "That it implies great changes when applied to the earth and heavens is very evident; but it never means annihilation, or the passing of things *out of being* . . . the main idea is transition, not extinction."[9]

The earth will be renovated. The key to understanding the renovation of the earth is Hebrews 1:12. In speaking of the present heaven and earth, it says, "Like a mantle You will roll them up; like a garment they will also be changed." The word "changed"[10] is used for "changing clothes." The same word is used in 1 Corinthians 15:51 where the bodies of believers are changed. The believer retains his identity, although he receives a glorified body. The earth remains "earth" though it is renovated and cleansed and becomes a "new earth." The analogy is important. As a believer is changed, receiving a glorified body, so the earth is changed into a new earth, unstained by sin.

Scriptures that speak of the earth being "completely laid waste and completely despoiled," "shaken violently" (Isa. 24:3, 19), and "burned up" (2 Pet. 3:10) emphasize a surface cleansing of the earth. These passages "may simply refer to its existence in its present form, not its very existence itself," Grudem notes.[11] Talbot adds, "The new earth will emerge from that baptism of elemental and judicial fire—clean, beautiful, holy. Every stain of sin, every mark of evil, will be wiped out. The condition of the earth as it was according to the record of Gen. 1:1 will be restored—with a 'plus.'"[12]

Peter paints another picture that helps us understand the renovation of the earth. He reminds us that the earth was once "destroyed, being flooded with water" (2 Peter 3:6) and that the second time it will be destroyed by fire. Was the earth annihilated when it was flooded in Noah's day? No. The earth was renovated. The evil of the earth was destroyed and removed; the earth was cleansed. Peter draws that analogy, saying it is "being reserved for fire, kept for the day of judgment and destruction of ungodly men" (v. 7). As in Noah's day, the earth was cleansed but not annihilated, so the earth will be cleansed but not annihilated in the conflagration that is to come. It will still exist as earth—but it will be the "new earth."

Peter is not describing "a total annihilation of the old earth and heaven" but a "remaking of them." Peter is describing a "renovation. It's like taking an old building and remodeling it."[13] An analogy is seen in the believer's body. Romans 8:30 tells us "those whom He justified, He also glorified." God didn't destroy us when He saved us nor will He destroy us when He glorifies us. It is this *same body* and *same person* that is glorified. Similarly, this *same earth* will be renovated but not destroyed.

A MAGNIFICENT RESTORATION AWAITS US

As Steve "Crocodile Hunter" Irwin and a TV crew were filming at the Great Barrier Reef in Australia, a stingray raised its tail, and its barbed spine pierced Irwin's heart. Irwin pulled the barb from his chest but lost consciousness and died shortly afterward.

Steve Irwin was well known for his love of wildlife preservation. Totally unafraid, Irwin confronted poisonous snakes and Komodo dragons and even stalked lions. But his trademark was hunting crocodiles in the outback of northern Australia, leaping on the back of a crocodile, grabbing its jaws, and tying its mouth shut. But nature isn't yet restored. This present earth is still in a fallen state. Nature is hostile. It awaits the renovation of the new earth.

The prophet Ezekiel pictures a future day when the earth will be restored: "This desolate land has become like the garden of Eden; and the waste, desolate and ruined cities are fortified and inhabited" (Ezek. 36:35). The connection of the restored earth with the ruined earth is evidenced in the garden of Eden. The original creation was magnificent in its unfallen, created state (Gen. 2:8). The earth will again be restored to Edenic conditions.

Isaiah, too, saw the future restored Eden: "Indeed, the Lord will comfort Zion; He will comfort all her waste places and her wilderness He will make like Eden, and her desert like the garden of the Lord" (Isa. 51:3). Isaiah foresaw the day when the desolate desert in Israel would be transformed to the original beauty of the unspoiled garden of Eden. He exclaimed, "The wilderness and the desert will be glad, and the Arabah [desert] will rejoice and blossom" (Isa. 35:1). How long? For a thousand years? No, longer—*forever*. In the same context Isaiah promised that the Israelites "shall possess it [the land] forever; from generation to generation they will dwell in it" (Isa. 34:17).

The effects of sin upon this earth will be removed; the new earth will again conform to God's original creation. And the glory of God will illuminate the earth (Isa. 35:2). The earth "must share in the final redemption. . . . Redemption includes the transformation of the earth . . . The future redeemed earth, though new, will no doubt have many continuities with the present earthly existence, yet without the violence, sorrow, pain, injustice, and the like that plague us."[14] On that day the earth will be cleansed. There will be no crime, no immorality, no evil of any kind.

THE CREATION ANTICIPATES
THE EARTH'S RESTORATION

Why do weeds grow more abundantly and rapidly than cultured plants? We don't have to fertilize weeds—they do very well on their own! Creation today is distorted and yearns for normality, according to the apostle Paul. He pictures a fallen creation as eagerly anticipating its restoration: "For the anxious longing of the creation waits eagerly for the revealing of the sons of God" (Rom. 8:19). The language is strong; creation is watching eagerly, as with outstretched hand, constantly and expectantly waiting until He comes who will restore all of creation.[15] Creation's anticipation for a renewed earth does not suggest an annihilation of the old earth.

Paul further writes: "For the creation was subjected to futility, not willingly, but because of Him who subjected it, in hope that the creation itself also will be set free from its slavery to corruption into the freedom of the glory of the children of God. For we know that the whole creation groans and suffers the pains of childbirth together until now" (Rom. 8:20–22). Just as an expectant mother gives birth to a healthy child, so creation is anticipating the day when it will be renewed in the freedom of God's glory. That is the appearance of the new earth, when all of nature will glorify God through the restored earth.

"Earth will be redeemed and resurrected," writes Randy Alcorn. "In the end it will be a far greater world. . . . It will preserve and perpetuate Earth's original design and heritage."[16]

CHRIST COMES IN JUDGMENT

Many believe that the earth will be restored and renovated at the end of the millennium; however, this should be reconsidered. Peter reminds us that the destruction of the present earth "will come like a thief" (2 Pet. 3:10). But this term ("*kleptes*") is normally used to describe the unexpected events at the second coming of Christ. Jesus warned that His coming would be unexpected, like the unexpected invasion of a thief (Matt. 24:43; Luke 12:39). Paul similarly reminds us of the horrific, unexpected destruction of the day of the Lord when Christ returns (1 Thess. 5:2). The church at Sardis was warned to repent, lest the Lord come unexpectedly, like a thief, to judge the church (Rev. 3:3). Following the bowl judgments in the tribulation, the Lord warns, "Behold, I am coming like a thief" (Rev. 16:15). Chronologically, the second coming of Christ is imminent when this announcement is made.

The description of the events at the second coming of Christ would also suggest the earth is renovated at the second coming. Joel describes the event: "Before them the earth quakes, the heavens tremble, the sun and the moon grow dark, and the stars lose their brightness" (Joel 2:10). He further says, "I will display wonders in the sky and on the earth, blood, fire, and columns of smoke" (Joel 2:30). Joel's description clearly fits the conflagration Peter describes. The fire, the smoke, the earth quaking—these all suggest the renovation of the earth is at the second coming of Christ. At that time the Lord will punish the earth for its evil and even the sun, moon, and stars will be affected (Isa. 13:10–11). The Lord punishing the earth suggests the renovation occurs at His second coming.

In another passage, Isaiah is even more descriptive: "And all the host of heaven will wear away, and the sky will be rolled up like a scroll"

TRUTHS ABOUT THE
NEW HEAVEN AND NEW EARTH

1 We will behold a new earth.
- *We will live on a restored earth.*
- *We will live on a productive land.*
- *We will live on a peaceful earth.*

2 Three elements mark a restored earth.
- *There is continuity.*
- *God's original purpose will be fulfilled.*
- *The earth will be renovated.*

3 A magnificent restoration awaits us.

4 The creation anticipates the earth's restoration.

5 Christ comes in judgment, then restoration.

6 Isaiah describes the renovation.

7 Joel describes the renovation.

8 Judgment is part of renovation.

9 The new heaven is on earth.

10 We should focus on the reality of the new earth.

(Isa. 34:4a). Isaiah 51:6 is similar: "For the sky will vanish like smoke, and the earth will wear out like a garment." Jesus announced that "heaven and earth will pass away" (Matt. 24:35). But He made the comment in the context of His second coming.

When Jesus comes in judgment (Matt. 24:33, 39), that is the time when the present heaven and earth will pass away. That day will come "like a thief" (2 Peter 3:10). As the *Theological Dictionary of the New Testament* notes, this simile emphasizes the sudden and unexpected aspects of Christ's return:

> In the NT *kleptes (kleptein)* [*"thief"*] is often used in parables or parabolic sayings for the breaking in of the Messianic age. . . . Paul uses the same comparison in 1 Thess. 5:2–4 when he is answering a question as to the time of the day of the Lord. He obviously builds on the dominical saying that the day of the Messiah will come as a thief at an unexpected hour. . . . The sudden and unexpected element in the day of the Lord is also brought out by the same figure in 2 Pt. 3:10."[17]

These references all seem to suggest the renovation of the earth occurs at the triumphant return of Christ at His second coming. It would also seem most natural that Christ will renovate and restore the earth to inaugurate His righteous rule when He establishes His kingdom at His second coming. Why would Christ rule over a debilitated, defiled, sin-stained earth? It is certainly more consistent and in concert with Scripture to suggest His righteous rule begins in a renovated and cleansed earth.

The words of Jesus in Matthew 24:43 suggest a sudden return, as does His warning to the church at Sardis: "Therefore if you do not wake up, I will come like a thief, and you will not know at what hour I will come to you" (Rev. 3:3). The similarity of language suggests the same event is referred to in all these references: Matthew 24:43; 2 Peter. 3:10; and Revelation 3:3.

When His disciples privately asked Him, "What will be the sign of Your coming, and of the end of the age?" Jesus referenced the prophet Joel and announced, "But immediately after the tribulation of those days the sun will be darkened, and the moon will not give its light, and the stars will fall from the sky, and the powers of the heavens will be shaken" (Matt. 24:3, 29).

In the context of the Olivet Discourse, Jesus has developed a chronology of the eschatological events. He has described the tribulation (vv. 4–28) and the signs of His second coming (vv. 29–31).

The destruction and renovation Jesus announced takes place at the second coming, when He comes to establish His eternal kingdom on earth. Jesus' announcement coincides with Zechariah's words (Zech. 14:6–7).

ISAIAH DESCRIBES THE RENOVATION

The day is coming when God will get the attention of all humanity— worldwide. God will shake the earth. In the context of establishing Christ's kingdom on earth, Isaiah graphically depicts the Lord's judgment and renovation of the earth: "The Lord lays the earth waste, devastates it, distorts its surface ... The earth will be completely laid waste and completely despoiled ... The earth mourns and withers, the world fades and withers ... The earth is broken asunder, the earth is split through, the earth is shaken violently. The earth reels to and fro like a drunkard and it totters like a shack ..." (Isa. 24:1, 3, 4, 19–20).

These are not mild words; this is no minor event. The graphic depiction portrays a total judgment of the earth and renovation of its surface. This is a judgment that impacts the entire earth. Delitzsch remarks, "It is a judgment which embraces all, without distinction of rank and condition; and it is a universal one ... in all the earth."[18] Herbert Wolf comments, "The destruction of the present heaven and earth in conjunction with Christ's second coming is described in Isaiah 24:19–23 and 34:4."[19]

When will this occur? These judgments reflect the judgments of the seal, trumpet, and bowl judgments of Revelation 6–19, culminating with the final judgment at the triumphant return of Jesus Christ (Rev. 19:11–21). Christ will both judge and cleanse the entire earth at His return. He will not rule in a blemished, sin-stained earth. He will rule in righteousness on a renovated earth.

JOEL DESCRIBES THE RENOVATION

In describing the Babylonian invasion of Judah, the prophet Joel transitions to the eschatological event of the earth's renovation: "Before them the earth quakes, the heavens tremble, the sun and moon grow dark and the stars lose their brightness" (Joel 2:10). This did not occur when the Babylonians invaded Judah. Joel has painted a portentous picture of the end of the age when God will shake the heavens and the earth. He later amplifies these comments in the context of the kingdom reign of Christ: "The sun and moon grow dark and the stars lose their brightness. The Lord roars from Zion and utters His voice from Jerusalem, and the heavens and the earth tremble" (Joel 3:15–16a).

On April 14, 2010, a volcano erupted near the Eyjafjoll Glacier in Iceland, creating an international disruption of air travel. The ash plumes rose to 30,000 feet, as the volcano discharged 750 tons of ash per second within the first three days. The ash and other airborne debris hampered visibility and threatened the large turbine engines of airplanes trying to maneuver around the volcanic residue that spread via the west-to-east jetstream. Airports and flight paths across the United Kingdom and European continent closed. Most transatlantic flights between North America and Europe were cancelled—some 63,000 flights in Europe and America. For one week, the air traffic snarl continued. People were stranded, and many ran out of funds as they could not return home. The European airlines alone lost more than one billion Euros.

One event. Dramatic consequences. These are but harbingers of what will occur in the last days.

Yet what follows is glorious. Joel describe the glory of the Messiah's reign in His kingdom on earth (Joel 3:17–21). "Mountains will drip with sweet wine . . . the hills will flow with milk, and all the brooks of Judah will flow with water" (v. 18).

ZECHARIAH DESCRIBES THE RENOVATION

In concert with Joel, Zechariah also describes the renovation of the heavens. He says, "In that day there will be no light; the luminaries will dwindle. For it will be a unique day which is known to the Lord, neither day nor night, but it will come about that at evening time there will be light" (Zech. 14:6–7). The language is strong. The sun, moon, and stars "will dwindle." Their light will "wane." As Merrill Unger explained, "There shall not be the light of the luminaries but thick murkiness" . . . The day of the Lord will be characterized by supernatural celestial disturbances."[20] God will shake not only the earth, but the universe—He will get humanity's attention!

The Lord will not destroy His original creation, but He will remove every defilement, every vestige of sin. It was here in the heavens that Lucifer rebelled (Isa. 14:12–17; Ezek. 28:11–19), and it is in these very same heavens that we will be cleansed before the Lord Jesus inaugurates His kingdom.

JUDGMENT IS PART OF RENOVATION

Clearly, final judgment is part of renovation—judgment of the Gentiles and all sinners and judgment of Lucifer, the great deceiver. The prophet Zephaniah pictures the glorious reign of Messiah on a purified earth. First the mighty King will judge the Gentile nations. The Lord says, "[I will] pour out on them My indignation, all My burning anger; for all the earth will be devoured by the fire of My zeal" (Zeph. 3:8). The language is graphic and inclusive. Christ the King will judge the earth for their rejection of His truth. But this is "not an exterminating but a refining judgment, through which [the Lord] will turn to the nations pure lips, to call upon His name."[21]

The earth will not be destroyed, but it will be cleansed; the entire earth will experience the renovating fire of the Lord. This will not be done in a corner; the Lord's judgment will cover the earth. "It is God's purpose to make the whole earth feel the full power of the divine anger against sin."[22]

Following the earth's cleansing, the people's hearts will be changed; they will worship the Lord with purified lips and serve Him (Zeph. 3:9). The description that follows pictures both the millennial and the new earth conditions (Zeph. 3:9–20). It is a *new earth*, cleansed and purified, upon which the Lord will rule over His people Israel and over the Gentile nations. Christ will rule over a *cleansed* earth, a peaceful earth.

The psalmist describes the tranquility of the new earth as "a river whose streams make glad the city of God" (Ps. 46:4; cf. Rev. 22:1). Yet that tranquil state will be accomplished when the Lord has "raised His voice, the earth melted" (Ps. 46:6; cf. Mic. 1:4). The Gentile nations are pictured in rebellion against the Lord as waters that roar and foam and mountains that quake with pride (Ps. 46:3, 6). But the Lord simply "raised His voice"—His voice thundered—and the earth dissolved. "The earth melted" is pictured as "melt[ing] with sweat."[23] As the Lord speaks, His will is done. Christ will rule as King in a cleansed earth when all evil is eradicated.

THE NEW HEAVEN IS ON EARTH

During Christ's millennial reign nothing contrary to righteousness will exist. You will find no liquor shops, night clubs, gambling casinos ... *ad infinitum* on the streets of the kingdom. Logic and, more importantly, Scripture indicates that all immorality will be removed at the inauguration of Christ's earthly kingdom.

The new heaven and the new earth are frequently pictured together

(Isa. 65:17; 66:22; 2 Peter 3:13; Rev. 21:1). Since God dwells with man on the new earth, and since God's home is heaven, the new earth becomes part of heaven. After that thousand years, we will live forever on the new earth. As Tim LaHaye summarizes, "The new earth will be the Christian's heaven."[24]

After the resurrection, believers will return to earth with Christ and reign with Him on earth during the millennium and then forever on the new earth. Here God's original purpose—fellowship with men and women in a perfect, sinless world— will be restored.

The Old Testament gives us considerable information concerning the new heaven, which will be developed in succeeding chapters. We normally disregard earthly kingdom passages as referring to heaven, but since "God will dwell with his people on the New Earth, these Scripture passages *do* refer to heaven."[25]

WE SHOULD FOCUS ON THE
REALITY OF THE NEW EARTH

We look at this earth and have the mistaken notion that this is the best—this is reality. Not so. This earth and everything in it is only a shadow of reality.

Helen and I had annual passes to Cypress Gardens in Florida for many years. We enjoyed walking through the historic gardens, seeing the beautiful flowers and trees, the immaculate landscaping—breathtaking! Surely this is unparalleled in beauty on earth: the blazing golden trumpet trees, the brilliant cascading bougainvillea, the majestic banyan tree spreading its long branches.

Gorgeous in beauty as Cypress Gardens is, it is only a *shadow* of the *reality* in the new heaven and the new earth. There we will feast our eyes on unparalleled beauty—indescribable beauty of the richest colors our eyes could behold. We will walk through the gardens of God that will make Cypress Gardens seem ordinary.

Abraham and the Old Testament heroes of the faith were "seeking a country of their own . . . they desire a better county, that is, a heavenly one" (Heb. 11:14, 16). Unquestionably, they saw beauty in their world, yet they knew there was a better world, a perfect, unblemished world. They set their hearts on the new earth, where heaven came down to unite with a renovated, glorious, unspoiled, unspeakably beautiful earth. This is what we should do.

While we will have failed in our tenure on the old earth, redeemed mankind will rule on the new earth with Christ (Rev. 22:5).[26] The tenure of that rule will not be restricted to a thousand years, but believers shall reign with Christ "forever and ever" (Rev. 22:5).

There we will worship the Lord and serve the Lord as we were purposed to do. On this new earth, cleansed and renovated—this eternal new earth—we will fulfill our eternal purpose for God. It is heaven on earth—*always better*. It is heaven revealed!

What will HEAVEN and the NEW EARTH Look Like?

Banff and Jasper National Parks in the Canadian Rockies had always been favorite places for Helen and me to visit. We honeymooned there and returned a number of times—always awestruck at the beauty. Seeing the majestic Mt. Norquay and Mt. Rundle in Banff, gazing upon the unspoiled majesty of the mountains and forests at Jasper always gave us joy and excitement.

Even in its fallen state, this earth is magnificent. How much more beautiful and majestic will the new heaven and the new earth be! We are limited by our imagination in picturing how glorious this new, renovated earth will be.

The sin of Adam and Eve changed everything, beginning with the once-pristine environment. When Adam disobeyed, God pronounced the disastrous effects of man's sin: "Cursed is the ground because of you; in toil you will eat of it all the days of your life. Both thorns and thistles it shall grow for you; and you will eat the plants of the field; by the sweat of your face you will eat bread" (Gen. 3:17b–19a). The earth changed. Life became difficult for Adam. The beautiful plants became resistant and troublesome. The ground did not readily yield produce. Instead, flood, drought, insects, and plagues would soon damage the plants and crops. And so it has been from the time of the first Adam until the day when the last Adam restores the earth to its God-ordained purpose.

God created this earth, and He called His creation "very good" (Gen. 1:31). This very earth must see a restoration to its pre-fall condition, to a perfect environment (Rom. 8:20–22). Satan caused the fall, but through the incarnation of Jesus Christ, Satan is a defeated foe. Redemption of humanity is only one aspect of Christ's victory. The restoration of this earth is also a part, an important part, of Christ's victory. This earth will see a renovation and renewal as the New Earth that will come down from heaven. A perfect environment will be the result. God, through Jesus Christ, is the victory, and the renewed earth will reflect that glory.

THE GLORY OF GOD WILL FILL THE EARTH

Early one morning, before the sun had risen, I got up and left the hotel in Tiberias, Israel. I had to climb over a tall stone fence in the back of the hotel, but then I was immediately at the shore of the Sea of Galilee. I stood there alone for a long period of time, watching the sun come up and cast its brilliant rays over the Sea of Galilee. I was awestruck at the beauty of the sun's glory reflected on the sea.

Imagine, though, how the glory of God will envelop the earth when Christ returns to rule in His kingdom and restore the earth. John reports, "And the city has no need of the sun or of the moon to shine on it, for the glory of God has illumined it, and its lamp is the Lamb" (Rev. 21:23). The sun is brilliant in its illumination; we cannot look into the sun or we will be blinded. Yet God's glory will illumine the earth in enormous brilliance that will far surpass the light of the sun. The light will emanate from the Jerusalem that has descended from heaven to the earth. "God's presence pervades the city and emits constant light in abundance."[1]

Moreover, "there will no longer be any night; and they will not have need of the light of a lamp nor the light of the sun, because the Lord God will illumine them" (Rev. 22:5). Darkness epitomizes evil. When Judas did his dastardly deed, Scripture says, "So after receiving the morsel he went out immediately; and it was night" (John 13:30). It is a blunt, cold statement. The darkness of the night depicts the darkness of Judas's deed. Evil lurks in darkness. Most crimes are committed during darkness. In that eternal day there will be no darkness, no night, no crime, no evil. The brilliant light emanating from the Lord will be a continual reminder of the light of God's truth and righteousness prevailing for all eternity.

Ezekiel describes the glory of God descending upon the earth in connection with the return of Jesus Christ: "And behold, the glory of the God of Israel was coming from the way of the east. And His voice was like the sound of many waters; and the earth shone with His glory" (Ezek. 43:2). In that day, Gentiles will recognize the holy God of Israel when His glory is illuminated universally (Ezek. 39:21).

Isaiah prophesied the glory of God emanating from Jerusalem, attracting the Gentile nations to come to the light (Isa. 60:1–3) that would envelop the earth: "No longer will you have the sun for light by day, nor for brightness will the moon give you light; but you will have the Lord for an everlasting light, and your God for your glory" (Isa. 60:19). In that day, the earth and the universe will be resplendent with God's illuminating brilliance.

THE NEW EARTH WILL BE LIKE EDEN

When God created the world, it was beautiful and perfect in every respect. The garden of Eden, unstained and untouched by sin, was perfect in beauty and in function. There Adam lived (Gen. 2:9) until his rebellion drove him out. The sin of Adam and Eve brought devastating effects upon the entire earth. But that is not the end of the story. God is not finished with the world. Christ, the Last Adam, will restore this earth to its perfect, pre-fall condition.

Remember, the new earth will be like Eden: "Indeed, the Lord will comfort Zion; He will comfort all her waste places. And her wilderness He will make like Eden," writes the prophet Isaiah, "and her desert like the garden of the Lord; joy and gladness will be found in her, thanksgiving and sound of a melody" (Isa. 51:3). Isaiah foresaw the new, Edenic earth. The deserts will be transformed into lush gardens. No more dusty desert and wasteland, the entire earth will be revisited to assume pre-fall Edenic glory.

THE TREE OF LIFE WILL BE ON EARTH

In His original creation, God placed the Tree of Life in the garden of Eden (Gen. 2:9). But when man sinned, God prevented him from eating of the tree lest he live forever in his sin (Gen. 3:22–24). Erwin Lutzer wisely states, "If Adam and Eve had eaten of the other special tree of the garden—the Tree of Life—they would have been immortalized in their sinful condition. They never would have qualified for the heaven that God wanted them to enjoy."[2]

But the Tree of Life will exist on the new earth, on both sides of the river, readily available for all to eat from (Rev. 22:2), as a continual reminder that the inhabitants are qualified as residents of the New Jerusalem and they will live forever (Rev. 22:14).

On this present, fallen earth there is sorrow, suffering, sickness, and death. On the new earth there will be life—everlasting life, unending health, joy, and gladness forever and ever. It is difficult to process this truth with our finite, mortal minds, but foundational to our basking in the glories of heaven is the Tree of Life. By its very existence we are promised an eternity of bliss in the presence of the glory of God.

THE RIVER OF LIFE WILL FLOW FOREVER

In the new heaven God will place a physical reminder of eternal, ongoing life. John is shown in the New Jerusalem "a river of the water of life, clear as crystal, coming from the throne of God and of the Lamb" (Rev. 22:1). Zechariah describes the same river flowing from Jerusalem to the Dead Sea and the Mediterranean Sea (14:8). Moreover, the river will flow in summer and in winter, a reminder that the waters will be "abundant and perennial."[3]

What is the meaning of the river of life? "These waters will be *literal* waters although they reflect and imply spiritual blessings," notes Unger.[4] The river in the New Jerusalem "speaks of the power, purity, and eternal life manifest in the heavenly city"[5] and the "fullness of life."[6] The presence of the river emphasizes the spiritual blessings and richness in the heavenly city. The river flows from the throne of God and of the Lamb, indicating that God Himself is the source of all the blessings, both physical and spiritual. The river of life is also a reminder of the river that "flowed out of Eden to water the garden" (Gen. 2:10).

THE DESERTS WILL GUSH WITH WATER

Water, the source of life, will be profuse and abundant on the new earth. Desert places will gush with water, "for waters will break forth in the wilderness [desert] and streams in the Arabah [desert]. The scorched land will become a pool and the thirsty ground springs of water" (Isa. 35:6b–7a). "The change of the desert into a field abounding with water is not a mere poetical ornament; for in the last times, the era of redemption, nature itself will really share in the *doxa* [glory] which proceeds from the manifested God to His redeemed."[7] Water, picturesque of God's redemption, will be in abundance (Isa. 41:18).

There are vast desert regions on this earth. North Africa is largely desert. Australia has an enormous desert region. The region south of Jerusalem is largely desert. Even the southwestern United States has three desolate deserts (the Chihuahuan, the Mojave, and the Sonoran). The deserts of the world depict the fall of nature (Genesis 3) and the reversal of the paradisiacal conditions of God's original creation.

But in the new earth, all nature will be restored as the waters transform the desert from desolate to lush. In that day, "the wilderness [desert] becomes a fertile field, and the fertile field is considered as a forest" (Isa. 32:15). The barren desert will be nonexistent. The badlands of South Dakota will teem with forests. The deserts of Arizona and California will flourish with green trees and abundant crops. The entire earth will be changed, transformed by the Lord, reflecting original Edenic beauty.

The desert is pictured as rejoicing at Messiah's eternal rule and blossoming in praise of Jesus Christ the King: "The wilderness and the desert will be glad, and the Arabah [desert] will rejoice and blossom" (Isa. 35:1). The creation that previously longed anxiously for its transformation (Rom. 8:19–22) now joyfully responds with rejoicing at its renovation. A new day has come. "The wilderness, the desert, the parched ground, the thirsty land, will all become fertile, for nature itself will reap the benefits of the removal of antagonistic powers, spiritual and human, and of the presence of the glory of the Lord and His people, earthly and heavenly."[8] Nature itself responds with "rejoicing and shout of joy" (Isa. 35:2) As the glory of God shall be evident in nature once more.

A BEAUTIFUL AND BOUNTIFUL LAND WILL FLOURISH

If we recognize the beauty and majesty of this present creation of a fallen world, how great, how beautiful will the creation on the new earth be? We have a hint from some of the prophets. Hosea declares,

PICTURES OF HEAVEN AND THE NEW EARTH

1 The glory of God will fill the earth.

2 The new earth will be like Eden.

3 The Tree of Life will be on the new earth.

4 The river of life will flow forever.

5 The deserts will gush with water.

6 A beautiful and bountiful land will flourish.

7 Animals will be plentiful and peaceful.

His shoots will sprout, and his beauty will be like the olive tree and his fragrance like the cedars of Lebanon. Those who live in his shadow will again raise grain, and they will blossom like the vine. His renown will be like the wine of Lebanon. (14:6–7)

Meanwhile, Joel prophesies:

So rejoice, O sons of Zion, and be glad in the Lord your God; for He has given you the early rain for your vindication and He has poured down for you the rain, the early and latter rain as before. The threshing floors will be full of grain, and the vats will overflow with the new wine and oil. . . . And in that day the mountains will drip with sweet wine, and the hills will flow with milk, and all the brooks of Judah will flow with water. (2:23–24; 3:18)

At that time creation will be set free from its bondage to corruption (cf. Rom. 8:20–22). The Lord will transform the earth. Isaiah promises, "Indeed, the Lord will comfort Zion; He will comfort all her waste places. And her wilderness He will make like Eden, and her desert like the garden of the Lord; joy and gladness will be found in her, thanksgiving and sound of a melody" (Isa. 51:3). The Lord will directly restore the earth, resulting in its perfection. What is the response? Shouting. Singing. Rejoicing. Redeemed men and women will celebrate the earth's transformation.

Not only will the land be beautiful, it will also be rich in productivity: "Then He will give you rain for the seed which you will sow in the ground, and bread from the yield of the ground, and it will be rich and plenteous; on that day your livestock will graze in a roomy pasture" (Isa. 30:23). God will provide precisely what the earth needs: rain to cause the crops to grow abundantly, resulting in a rich and abundant yield. Livestock has room to graze with more than sufficient food. A glorious picture of the glory of God bathing the world in luxurious beauty.

Ezekiel paints for us the picture of a bountiful land: "Also the tree of the field will yield its fruit and the earth will yield its increase, and they will be secure on their land" (Ezek. 34:27). The prophet reminds us that the crops on the new earth will be in far greater abundance than on the old earth. Farmers will harvest gigantic crops of wheat, oats, barley, and rye. Those tending vineyards will have grapes overflowing (Isa. 65:21), and orchardists will enjoy an abundance of oranges, cherries, apples—a great harvest of fruit. In every sphere the crops will be abundant.

When we moved to Florida's Tampa Bay area, Helen planted two orange trees. Helen had a green thumb, and she knew how to nurture plants. It wasn't long before the temple orange trees grew and began to produce oranges. After just a few years we had a bountiful crop. I'm a counter, and when Helen began to pick the oranges, I reminded her to keep track of the number of oranges, so she faithfully wrote down the number of oranges she picked. She filled the bathtub in the spare bathroom with oranges—over 1,400 oranges from two trees! And temple oranges are wonderfully juicy without pulp. But now imagine—if we can enjoy a great crop of oranges like that in a fallen world, what will the crop of oranges (and other fruit, vegetable, and grain products) be on the new earth?

There will be no diseases, no insects, no droughts, no floods to hinder the crops. Solomon confirms this: "May there be abundance of grain in the earth on top of the mountains; its fruit will wave like the cedars of Lebanon" (Ps. 72:16). Solomon sees the fruit trees waving like the tall cedar trees. A beautiful picture of the productive crops.

Farmers normally let their land lie dormant for one year after four or five years of harvesting crops on a particular field so the land can regain its strength and be productive again. Not so on the new earth. The land will be productive continuously—forever. Isaiah promises, "For as the lifetime of a tree, so will be the days of My people" (Isa. 65:22b). What are the "days of My people"? Forever. Those who enter the millennium in their mortal bodies will enjoy longevity (cf. Isa. 65:20), but so will God's creation. There will be no shriveled plants or trees. No dried leaves scattered across lawns. Trees will be green continuously; plants will blossom with blazing colors regularly.

Imagine then, this entire earth, from the deserts of Arizona to the barren poverty of Africa and the desolation of Siberia. The entire earth will be transformed; every corner of earth will depict the Lord's glorious transformation of the earth into an abundant, Eden-like paradise.

ANIMALS WILL BE PLENTIFUL AND PEACEFUL

When the American West was opening to settlers in the 1800s, buffalo roamed the plains in countless numbers—thousands upon thousands.

Tragically, hunters decimated the numbers so that buffalo became an endangered species. Before hunters invaded the interior of Africa, wildlife was abundant there as well. Modern man has decimated the animals on this earth—but that is not the end of the story.

A day is coming when animals will freely roam this earth unhindered, in large herds and flocks. Isaiah promises, "On that day your livestock will graze in a roomy pasture. Also the oxen and the donkeys which work the ground will eat salted fodder, which has been winnowed with shovel and fork" (Isa. 30:23b–24). Farmers will again enjoy their livestock (Isa. 61:5). Conditions will be perfect, with the animals enjoying expansive pastures (Isa. 30:23). Even the animals themselves will enjoy the bounty of the new earth in their fodder (Isa. 30:24). And they will have room to roam (Isa. 32:20).

I was always fascinated by the moose—that majestic animal with its huge antlers—but I have observed the moose only at a distance. On that future day animals will be nearby—and they will be at peace with mankind. On the new earth, Isaiah prophesied:

> The wolf will dwell with the lamb, and the leopard will lie down with the young goat, and the calf and the young lion and the fatling together; and a little boy will lead them. Also the cow and the bear will graze, their young will lie down together, and the lion will eat straw like the ox. The nursing child will play by the hole of the cobra, and the weaned child will put his hand on the viper's den. They will not hurt or destroy in all My holy mountain. (Isa. 11:6–9a)

In that day animals that don't naturally live together on this earth will live together on that earth. At present, the wolf and lamb don't coexist peacefully on this earth—the lamb wouldn't survive. The leopard and goat don't belong together, nor the lion and calf, nor the cow and bear. But there will be entire peace in the animal kingdom. All animals will coexist in peace—with humanity. A little boy will scratch the neck of a lion without fear and will play with a snake unharmed. The vicious animals of today will be the tame animals tomorrow: "'They will do no evil or harm in all My holy mountain,' says the Lord" (Isa. 65:25b).

The new earth will complete God's program. It will be what God intended for Adam and Eve in Eden. This earth reflects the Lord's beauty, but the new earth will exceed the beauty of this earth. God's glory will envelop the new earth with its spectacular scenery, with the animal world living in total peace. The animals' ferocity will be gone; they will be tame and peaceful.

This glorious new earth will look like Eden restored, the new earth as God designed it, where it is *always better in every way.* It is heaven revealed!

What will LIFE Be Like

in HEAVEN?

I think of the polio epidemic that hit Manitoba, Canada, first in the mid 1950s, and again in the later 1960s. A lovely teenage girl in our high school died of the dreaded disease during the first outbreak. In the 1960s a young married woman didn't die of polio, but she was totally incapacitated, confined to living the remainder of her life in an iron lung. She had no independent bodily function whatsoever; she couldn't even breathe on her own.

Sometimes I am overwhelmed when I read our prayer requests in our Wednesday church bulletin: heart surgery, multiple sclerosis, stroke, cancer, death—the list is endless. Sickness and death are constant visitors to our homes. We all have or will encounter physical suffering in this life.

On this sinful, fallen earth, life will remain difficult, fraught with suffering and sadness. But we are looking forward to *heaven*—and heaven is always better in every realm than the earth. We should never question, doubt, or worry whether we will "enjoy" heaven. We will enjoy heaven *to the utmost;* every moment in heaven will be better than the best moments we ever have on this fallen earth. The suffering on this earth will be a thing of the past—*forever.*

JOY AND HAPPINESS AWAIT IN HEAVEN

If we were to describe happiness, we would probably restrict it to a particular event or moment: getting a raise, a child being born healthy, our football team scoring the winning touchdown, going on a trip to a special place ... but unquestionably, our joy is limited, not constant. It exists for a moment, and then comes the normality of life involving some discouraging news or simply the humdrum of daily life, fraught with problems and perhaps work, that is boring.

Heaven will consist of constant, unending joy and happiness. Can we even fathom that? Isaiah says believers will "come with joyful shouting to Zion, and everlasting joy will be on their heads. They will obtain gladness and joy, and sorrow and sighing will flee away" (Isa. 51:11). God invites us to "shout joyfully together" (Isa. 52:9).

Jesus reminds us, "Blessed are you who weep now, for you shall laugh" (Luke 6:21b). The description is vivid. The phrase "you who weep" (a present participle) emphasizes the continual weeping. Does this happen? Sadly, it does. My mother became a widow at age forty-six, and I clearly recall her sitting at home Sunday afternoons and weeping. My parents had a great marriage, and although my mother lived as a widow until age eighty-nine, she never got over my father's death. She wept a lot.

But there is a future day when those who weep will laugh. And it will be a genuine, joyful, divinely initiated laughter—God will cause them to laugh.[1] And they will *never* mourn or cry again.

It's a beautiful picture. In heaven the joy will be so intense it will involve shouting—and it will be unending—it is "everlasting." Think of your most wonderful moment and then extend that, not for a day, a month, a year, but forever. Endless joy. Endless happiness. In fact, since we will continuously be growing in our knowledge of God for all eternity, may it not be that we will also grow in our joy?

In all that we do in heaven—and we will be active—our lives will be filled with joy. It is so evident that even the mountains and hills are heard shouting and the trees are pictured as clapping their hands (Isa. 55:12). David says, "You make the dawn and the sunset shout for joy" (Ps. 65:8). The brilliant beams of sunshine streaking across the earth illustrate the joy and happiness that await believers in glory. All of nature—restored nature on the new earth—will rejoice. God has created His people for joy and happiness. That was His purpose for Adam and Eve and their posterity, but they forfeited joy because of their sin in the garden. But the story isn't over. God will write the final chapter and that will include restored joy. The joy that Adam lost will be restored on the new earth.

In that future day we will rejoice at God's creation of the new earth (Isa. 65:17–18). All of the issues, all of the things that result in sadness and crying on this fallen earth will be gone. There will be only joy and gladness.

The central focus of our joy and gladness in glory will be the presence of the Lord Himself: "Sing for joy and be glad, O daughter of Zion; for behold I am coming and I will dwell in your midst" (Zech. 2:10). The presence of the Lord will create joy and gladness that will be expressed in joyful singing. In His presence we will experience pleasures beyond description, happiness that exceeds anything on this earth. And we will experience that joy and happiness constantly, forever (Ps. 16:11).

RESTORED HEALTH AWAITS IN HEAVEN

Fanny Crosby was only six weeks old when a man claiming to be a physician placed a hot poultice on her eyes to remove an infection. Instead, the would-be remedy blinded her. Fanny Crosby came to be a noted hymn writer but she never regained her sight, although she lived to be ninety-five. Isaiah reminds us of that new day: "Then the eyes of the blind will be opened and the ears of the deaf will be unstopped. Then the lame will leap like a deer, and the tongue of the mute will shout for joy" (35:5–6). There is coming a future day, both in the millennium and in the eternal state on the new earth, when illnesses will cease. There will be no more blindness, no people in wheelchairs, no illness of any kind. Therapists will be out of business.

There is a glorious day coming when "out of their gloom and darkness the eyes of the blind will see" (Isa. 29:18; cf. 32:3). There will be no blindness in heaven, not even glasses or contact lenses. Ophthalmologists and optometrists will also be out of business. There will be no hearing aids. Crutches will be nonexistent. No one will have slurred speech. We will all have sharp minds; we will know more than we ever knew on earth, and we will discern truth (Isa. 32:4).

Our senses will be perfect. We will see perfectly—and there will be pristine beauty to see; we will hear sounds we have never heard before; we will speak without mumbling or hesitancy; we will walk and jump with joy and vitality. No illness, no pain—instead we will enjoy the perfection of our glorified bodies, and we will continue in that state unabated, forever (Mic. 4:6–7). There will never again be deterioration in our health in any form.

PROSPERITY AND SECURITY ARE OURS IN HEAVEN

One Sunday morning when my cousin was a teenager, he and a friend drove to a farmhouse and went inside. In those days people didn't lock their doors. The farmer and his family were in church. But my cousin smelled the chicken cooking in the kitchen, and he and his friend made themselves at home and helped themselves. They took the chicken out of the oven, sat down, and enjoyed a chicken dinner at the farmer's expense!

WHAT WILL LIFE BE LIKE?

1 Joy and happiness await in heaven.

2 Restored health awaits in heaven.

3 Prosperity and security are ours in heaven.

4 We will enjoy banquets in heaven.

5 We will live in peace and safety.

6 We will no longer cry, feel sad, or face death.

7 We will recognize each other.

8 Our body will be perfect, locked into eternal youth.

10 Our perception of family members will be unique.

11 Only those who believe Jesus is the Christ will be there.

Times have changed. People do indeed lock their doors today. Most have a security system, dead bolt locks, and, if living in a high-crime area, sometimes barred windows. Criminals and vandals force home-owners to take numerous precautions to protect themselves and their property from theft and destruction.

But there is a new picture on the new earth: "Each of them will sit under his vine and under his fig tree, with no one to make them afraid, for the mouth of the Lord has spoken" (Mic. 4:4). The new earth will enjoy continual prosperity and security. There will be no cause for fear. No one will be in heaven to create fear, and no one in heaven will be afraid of anyone.

On the new earth people will enjoy prosperity; the vine and fig tree represent abundance and suggest that believers will have the peaceful environment in which they will enjoy their abundance. They will have time and relaxation with loved ones, friends, and neighbors to be refreshed from their orchards. "In that day ... every one of you will invite his neighbor to sit under his vine and under his fig tree" (Zech. 3:10). It will be a time of "peace and prosperity";[2] it will be a time of restful fellowship in a perfect environment with friends and loved ones. Believers will enjoy "the good life" in glory.

WE WILL ENJOY BANQUETS

Will we eat in heaven? There is no question. Isaiah paints a picture of a sumptuous banquet: "The Lord of hosts will prepare a lavish banquet for all peoples on this mountain; a banquet of aged wine, choice pieces with marrow, and refined, aged wine" (Isa. 25:6). Isaiah pictures Gentiles, people from all nations, coming to "this mountain"—Jerusalem —for a grand banquet, celebrating the Lord's rule over the kingdoms of the world.

The celebration and banqueting begins with the inauguration of the millennial kingdom (Rev. 19:9), but the context of Isaiah indicates the banqueting continues into the eternal state, on the new earth. I don't know whether the feast will include T-bone steaks, shrimp and scallops, or lasagna. I do know that the prophet Joel envisioned the day when "you will have plenty to eat and be satisfied and praise the name of the Lord your God, Who has dealt wondrously with you" (Joel 2:26).

Jesus Himself told of the future day when "many will come from east and west, and recline at the table with Abraham, Isaac and Jacob in the kingdom of heaven" (Matt. 8:11). Jesus' miracles of feeding the multitudes was a foreshadowing of the lavish banquet in the kingdom of heaven (Matt. 14:13–21; 15:32–39). When Jesus fed the multitudes, "they all ate and were satisfied" (Matt. 15:37). "Satisfied" (Gk. *perisseuon*) means "to be in abundance, to be in excess."[3] It points to Jesus' lavish provision for His people and is a reminder that in heaven—on the new earth—believers will not only dine, they will dine in abundance. There will be no Weight Watchers menu or "over fifty-five" reduced-price menu, no "healthy food" section. All will enjoy the sumptuous provision of the King for all eternity.

Jesus pictured kingdom life as a wedding feast, lavishly prepared: "Behold, I have prepared my dinner; my oxen and my fattened livestock are all butchered and everything is ready; come to the wedding feast" (Matt. 22:4). This passage, as many others, refers to the millennial kingdom but, as is common, reverberates with life on the new earth in the eternal state. But that also raises questions of whether we will eat meat in heaven. Eating meat requires death. Animals will be slaughtered in the millennial kingdom, but it is unlikely there will be death of animals on the new earth in the eternal state. Yet the promise of Isaiah 25:6 that we will eat "choice pieces with marrow" may mean we will eat meat, since the term is used for the fat of animals (Ps. 66:15).[4] How? God is not limited; He is capable of providing meat without the sacrifice of animals.

What else will be on the menu? We do know that we will eat fruit in heaven (Rev. 22:2). We also know that eating is possible in our resurrection bodies since Christ ate a breakfast of bread and fish with the disciples after He was resurrected (John 21:12, 13). Perhaps we will dine on salmon, grouper, and trout! Jesus promised those who hunger in this age will "be satisfied" in the age to come (Luke 6:21). "Be satisfied" (*chortasthesesthe*) is an unusually strong term, meaning "to eat one's fill" and is used of animals and also birds gorging themselves (Rev. 19:21).[5] The picture is evident. In the millennium and on the new earth we will banquet sumptuously.

WE WILL LIVE IN PEACE AND SAFETY

Whether swimming in the Gulf of Mexico or in the Atlantic Ocean, Florida residents have learned to be wary of shark attacks. Once a man from St. Petersburg dove off the dock into the Gulf and was immediately hit and killed by a shark. Apparently his sudden entry into the water had startled the shark, and the shark attacked him. But danger from the animal world is not restricted to Florida.

During one visit to Banff National Park, Helen and I came in contact (not too close) with black bears, elk, and moose—all of which were capable (and willing) to inflict harm on us. On one occasion I was wandering alone in the woods behind the condo, and I saw an elk standing in the open. *What a great picture*! I thought. So I went farther into the open toward the elk and focused my camera. And he charged me! I remembered what I had heard about elks and ran to the nearest tree and stood still behind it, and the elk stopped!

The animal world is not at peace with mankind. Since God put the fear of man in animals (Gen. 9:2), they have been at enmity and will remain so until the kingdom age dawns. God has promised, "In that day I will also make a covenant for them with the beasts of the field, the birds of the sky and the creeping things of the ground. And I will abolish the bow, the sword and war from the land, and will make them lie down in safety" (Hos. 2:18). Just as God put the fear of man in the animals, to protect the animals, so in that future day God will make a new covenant and bring total peace to the animal world. Rattlesnakes, black widow spiders, sharks, cougars, lions, and tigers will all live in peace with humanity. When Christ establishes His kingdom, not only will humanity be at peace, but the entire environment, the animal world and nature itself will be at peace.

God has promised, "'The wolf and the lamb will graze together, and the lion will eat straw like the ox; and dust will be the serpent's food. They will do no evil or harm in all My holy mountain,' says the

Lord" (Isa. 65:25). Earlier in Isaiah God declared, "Behold, I create new heavens and a new earth" (65:17). John also mentions the new heaven and the new earth in the context of eternity, after the millennium (Rev. 21:1). We can confidently conclude that these conditions will continue beyond the millennium and for all eternity.

For all eternity, on the new earth, we will enjoy the glory of God's creation in nature; the lion and wolf will be tame, inflicting no harm. Lambs will graze peacefully without fear of a vicious, wild animal. Poisonous snakes will be poisonous no more. Even a child (if childhood extends into the eternal state) will peacefully play with a cobra or viper (Isa. 11:8). The reason? Humanity, the animal world, and all of nature will be subservient to the Lord. Everyone and everything will have a knowledge of the Lord (Isa. 11:9). There will be a return to "the conditions of Paradise."[6] It is "Paradise Lost—Paradise Regained." What Adam lost, Christ will regain.

WE WILL NO LONGER CRY, FEEL SAD, OR FACE DEATH

Helen and I had a phenomenal marriage for forty-five years, truly wedded in soul, heart, and mind. She would muse, "One of us can start the sentence, and the other can finish it." And so it was. We were truly one.

Since January 31, 2005, I have shed more tears than I had shed in my entire life prior. Helen's sudden homegoing tore my heart like nothing ever has or ever will. But God has promised that there is a glorious, future day coming when no one will ever again shed a single tear. God has promised that in the new heaven and new earth, "He will wipe away every tear from their eyes; and there will no longer be any death; there will no longer be any mourning, or crying, or pain; the first things have passed away" (Rev. 21:4).

Everyone, without exception, will at some point shed tears because of sickness and death. At a certain time, some illness or accident will eventually overtake us and, barring the Lord's return, will lead to the grave. As my philosophical mother-in-law would say matter-of-factly: "Well, I have to die of something!"

The Scripture promises that glorious, future day when no more tears will be shed: "He will swallow up death for all time, and the Lord God will wipe tears away from all faces" (Isa. 25:8a). Since there will be death in the millennium, this must take place beyond the millennium and describe heaven, our eternal state on the new earth. Mankind's greatest enemy—death—will be eliminated. Jesus Christ has accomplished this: "Christ Jesus, who abolished death and brought life and immortality to light through the gospel" (2 Tim. 1:10). The word "abolished" means to "render inoperative, to make inactive, to annul."[7] What a glorious truth and what a joyous day that will be! The funeral home industry will close up shop. *Pallbearers* will be a forgotten word. No longer will anyone hear the sound of someone else crying (Isa. 65:19). Tears will terminate.

That future eternal day on the new earth will see the ultimate fulfillment of the promise of the beatitude, "Blessed are those who mourn, for they shall be comforted" (Matt. 5:4). That day will usher in the ultimate comfort. In that day there will be "*everlasting* joy" when "sorrow and sighing will flee away" (Isa. 51:11). No more crying. Ever. The Lord Himself shall prevail over every vestige of evil. He will dry our tears and provide tranquility. That peaceful state will be ours to enjoy and bask in with our saved loved ones *forever*. The tears you and I shed now are temporary. They will not continue. One glorious day God will dry all our tears as He ushers in His day of eternal peace and joy.

WE WILL RECOGNIZE EACH OTHER

When Jesus promised His disciples, "I will not drink of this fruit of the vine from now on until that day when I drink it new with you in My Father's kingdom," He indicated that their identities would continue

(Matt. 26:29). When He spoke of "I" and "you," He implied that there would be a continuity in both Himself and the disciples. They would recognize Him as the One with whom they had fellowship during His earthly existence, and He would recognize them as the eleven with whom He had fellowship. It was a clear statement that their identities and distinctiveness would continue on in heaven for eternity.

Identity distinguishes the person. We are who we are through our identities. If we had different identities, our personhood would not be distinguishable. We would be unrecognizable. In the wonderful promise of John 3:16, God promises eternal life to "whoever" believes in Him. The individual "whoever" receives "eternal life." The language demands that the very identity of the individual who believes will live on forever in heaven. And that individual will be identifiable by his or her character traits.

"What makes you *you*?" asks Randy Alcorn. "It's not only your body but also your memory, personality traits, gifts, passions, preferences, and interests. In the final resurrection, I believe all of these facets will be restored and amplified, untarnished by sin and the Curse."[8]

I'll see and recognize Helen. I'll see her infectious smile, her excitement, her curiosity, her sharp mind and insight, and especially her love. You will recognize your loved ones, and your fellowship will continue in a greater dimension, unabated. It will never end. What a glorious thought!

OUR BODY WILL BE PERFECT, LOCKED INTO ETERNAL YOUTH

What did Adam and Eve look like before the fall? Unquestionably, they were perfect. They were young-looking and sinless; they would have been breathtakingly beautiful, perfect in every sense. Only with the fall did the disintegration of the human body begin.

In eternity, we will have bodies that are eternally youthful and beautiful. Augustine said the body "shall be of that size which it either had attained or should have attained in the flower of its youth, and shall enjoy the beauty that arises from preserving symmetry and proportion in all its members . . . overgrown and emaciated persons need not fear that they shall be in heaven of such a figure as they would not be even in this world if they could help it."[9]

British theologian Alister McGrath says that by the late thirteenth century the church concluded:

> "As each person reaches their peak of perfection around the age of 30, they will be resurrected, as they would have appeared at that time—even if they never lived to reach that age." Peter Lombard's discussion of the matter is typical of his age: "A boy who dies immediately after being born will be resurrected in that form which he would have had if he had lived to the age of thirty." The New Jerusalem will thus be populated by men and women as they would appear at the age of 30 . . . but with every blemish removed.[10]

Thomas Aquinas said that we would all be approximately thirty-three, the age of perfection, the age of Jesus Christ when He was crucified.[11]

Hank Hanegraaff says, "Our DNA is programmed in such a way that, at a particular point, we reach optimal development from a functional perspective. For the most part, it appears that we reach this stage somewhere in our twenties and thirties. . . . If the blueprints for our glorified bodies are in the DNA, then it would stand to reason that our bodies will be resurrected at the optimal stage of development determined by our DNA."[12]

OUR PERCEPTION OF FAMILY MEMBERS
WILL BE UNIQUE

How will we view our spouses, parents, and children? While we agree that we will all have ideal, ageless bodies, locked into a youthful perception of age, we will probably see each other according to our earthly relationships.

Randy Alcorn says, "I suggest the possibility that in Heaven we'll see people as we most remember them on earth. So I'll see my parents as older, and they'll see me as younger. I'll see my children as younger, and they'll see me as older. I don't mean that physical forms will actually change but that the resurrection body will convey the real person we have known, and we will see each other through different eyes."[13]

THOSE WHO BELIEVE JESUS
IS THE CHRIST WILL BE THERE

The admission to heaven is through faith in Jesus Christ. He is the only way. There is no other philosophy, no religion, no other way that will get you to heaven. But by trusting in Jesus Christ alone, recognizing He died on the cross to pay the penalty for your sins, you can be assured that when you leave this earth, you will simply transition to heaven. Then the real you will never die. Jesus said, "Everyone who lives and believes in Me will never die" (John 11:26). That is the invitation to you.

And as a believer, you need not fear death. Your last breath on earth will be your first breath in heaven—and then life truly begins!

This phenomenal, glorious, endless life in heaven is for those who believe Jesus is the Christ sent to redeem mankind. If you have never trusted in Jesus Christ, come to Him in faith and receive the gift of eternal life. If you are a believer, look forward with joyful anticipation to the glorious future that awaits you and me. It is heaven—*always better*—*it is heaven revealed!*

What Is the CONTINUITY Between This Life and Life in HEAVEN?

When we think about heaven we ask many questions. Does this life have any relationship with heaven? How will I function—will I be the same individual or will I be different? Will the things I do on this earth have any relationship with what I do and how I live in heaven? What will my relationships be like in heaven? Will I remember the things that took place on this earth—things that I did—will I remember them?

Questions, questions—we have a lot of questions about heaven. The underlying question is: What is the continuity of this life with heaven? That is the issue we will now address.

OUR EARTHLY BODIES CONTINUE, BUT AS GLORIFIED BODIES

Will there be a continuity of our old earth bodies to our bodies on the new earth? Some may not want to hear a positive answer to that question! But a foundational truth is that *all of us* will have glorified bodies.

There will be *no* imperfections in heaven on the new earth. Every body will be perfect—yet distinct and different from each other. Our bodies, while sown in dishonor, will be "raised in glory . . . raised in power . . . raised a spiritual body" (1 Cor. 15:43–44). Could there be imperfections or inadequacies? No. Distinctly no.

How will there be a continuity of this old earthly body? After all, some of us are too thin or too thick, too short or too tall. What about baldness? Some of us would like to change our looks or appearance. Will we appear in heaven as we do here on this earth?

We know for certain that we will have physical bodies, and they will be bodies in continuity with our old earth bodies. Jesus made numerous appearances to the eleven remaining disciples, to the women, and to many others—and they recognized Him as the Jesus they had known before the resurrection. When Mary was weeping at the tomb, Jesus called her by name, "Mary!" (John 20:16). She immediately recognized Him; after all, she would have heard Him call her by name many times. The tone of His voice addressing her as "Mary" was familiar. It was the same voice—it was the same Jesus!

When the ten disciples told Thomas about seeing the resurrected Savior, he disputed their claim. But when Christ appeared to Thomas, inviting him to touch His nail-pierced hand and side, Thomas recognized Jesus (John 20:28). Yes, there was a continuity of the body of Jesus—He retained the nail prints in His hands and the spear's wound in His side. Unquestionably, this is important and valuable. It will be an eternal reminder for us that we are in heaven because of the price Jesus paid on our behalf.

Jesus' resurrection body was just that—*a body.* And it was a body of continuity with His body prior to His resurrection. They recognized Him. It was the same Jesus! And it will be the same you and me—with our distinct bodies (without any defect!).

OUR DISTINCTIVE PERSONALITIES WILL CONTINUE

God created man and woman—uniquely so. Men and women think in distinct ways, and in that they complement each other. Why are men and women attracted to each other? Because of their distinct personalities. I will forever remember my first meeting with Helen. Her sparkling eyes and cheerful smile, her happy disposition captured me immediately. And that's who Helen was throughout her life—cheerful and happy. What will Helen be like in heaven? Cheerful and happy! We will retain our distinctive characteristics—that is who we are.

However, there will be no negative features to our personalities, even though we all have them on earth. Instead, we will be perfect, complete in every sense. When we receive our resurrection bodies, we receive not only glorified bodies, we also receive transformed and glorified minds. Our entire person—body, soul, and spirit—is transformed, but we retain our distinctive characteristics. Isn't that a wonderful thought?

That should answer one question someone may raise—what about someone who is prone to depression? Will my spouse, my son, my friend exhibit depression in heaven? No. Remember, there will be no negative features in heaven; otherwise it wouldn't be heaven. Yes, we will retain our unique personalities but without negative aspects. We will have our distinct personalities. Sir William Robertson Nicoll said, "Our personalities are distinct in the next world, and that a pure and holy love between individuals in this life is a creation of God, and will live on in the next."[1] Oswald Sanders added, "The essential element of personality . . . will persist after death."[2]

God made us as distinct individuals and we will retain that uniqueness—that marvelous creation of God, distinguishing us as *individuals.*

We aren't given details about Moses and Elijah when they appeared at Jesus' transfiguration, nonetheless, they appeared *as Moses and Elijah*

(Matt. 17:1ff). Moses and Elijah were two very distinct personalities in the Old Testament. As Peter, James, and John listened to them talking with Jesus, they must have said some things that made the three recognize them. In other words, there was a continuity of their personalities with these reflected in their lives in the Old Testament.

Scripture is clear: There is a continuity of this earthly personality and body with the personality and body that we will have in the resurrection on the new earth. That has many implications. We will continue the relationships with the people we loved on this earth. The fellowship will be enormous—but we won't be limited by time constraints! Erwin Lutzer reminds us that "our personalities continue. . . . Heaven is the earthly life of the believer glorified and perfected."[3] What a wonderful prospect!

OUR MEMORIES OF PEOPLE
AND EVENTS WILL CONTINUE

When Abraham spoke to the rich man in hades, he said, "Child, remember that during your life you received your good things" (Luke 16:25). Abraham's admonition was for the rich man to "remember." And the rich man did remember. He remembered his family, how many brothers he had, their spiritual need . . . and much more. The point is clear. If the people in hell will remember their past lives on this earth, surely believers in heaven will remember their lives on earth. Abilities in heaven will not be inferior to abilities in hell.

There will be a continuity of our memory with our lives and events on this earth when we are in heaven. We will remember. "One minute after we die, our minds, our memories, will be clearer than ever before," Lutzer writes. "Our personalities will just go on with the same information we have stored in our minds today. Think back to your background: your parents, brothers, sisters, family reunions. Of course, you will remember all of this and more in heaven. Do you actually think you might know less in heaven than you do on earth? Unthinkable!"[4]

Yes, we will know one another in heaven.[5] In heaven you will know your believing parents who have gone ahead; you will know your husband, your wife, your children, your parents, your friends.

For all eternity we will be able to share memories and recall past events with family members and friends. I suspect Helen will recall a rather bizarre event from our honeymoon. We were at Lake Louise in the Rocky Mountains in western Canada, where I suggested we take a horseback ride around the lake. Helen was reticent since she had negative experiences with horses in her childhood at the family farm. But she finally agreed when I asked the attendant to provide the most timid horse for Helen. Soon we were on horseback, riding around Lake Louise. Workmen had placed a water hose from the lake across the path where we were riding. As Helen neared the water hose, there was a water surge, and the hose lurched up and down.

Helen's horse was spooked; it bolted and raced back to camp with a terrified honeymoon bride holding on to the reins for dear life. The attendants, on horseback, had to chase down the horse and bring it to a halt. Helen never rode a horse again. I suspect that story will be remembered and rehearsed!

But there is one significant difference with our memories in heaven: My family and yours will remember one another more fully. Scripture says, "For now we see in a mirror dimly, but then face to face; now I know in part, but then I will know fully just as I also have been fully known" (1 Cor. 13:12). We will know everything we know now, but much clearer and much more. On that day we will have a greater knowledge of God than we have today[6] and with that, a greater knowledge of each other. The prospect of that sublime truth should provoke us to keep focused on heaven.

OUR RELATIONSHIPS WITH
EACH OTHER WILL CONTINUE

When John Derksen, my friend from grade school, comes to see me, we continue our fellowship as though we had seen each other yesterday—even though we haven't seen each other for a year. Undoubtedly, that is a preview of how it will be in heaven. We will take up and continue our relationships with family and friends as though we had seen each other yesterday—only the fellowship will be greater than anything we enjoyed on the old earth—no matter how good it was.

Will we be closer or more distant with our loved ones in heaven? "What we do here touches strings that reverberate for all eternity. . . . I fully expect no one besides God will understand me better on the New Earth, and there's nobody whose company I'll seek and enjoy more than Nanci's," writes Randy Alcorn in his book *Heaven.* "Jesus . . . never hinted that deep relationships between married people would end."[7] When Abraham died, the Scripture recounts, "Abraham breathed his last and died . . . and he was gathered to his people" (Gen. 25:8). Who were "his people"? Sarah, first of all, then other family members. The whole point of being "gathered to his people" is that there is reunion with loved ones in heaven and that we will know each other and have eternal, unending fellowship with each other. Won't that be sublime?

For those who have lost a family member, recall the promise of the apostle Paul. As he comforted the grieving Thessalonians concerning those who had died, he reminded them of the glorious reunion of believers at the rapture: "The dead in Christ will rise first. Then we who are alive and remain will be caught up together with them in the clouds to meet the Lord in the air, and so we shall always be with the Lord" (1 Thess. 4:16b–17). This is a reminder that at the rapture those who are alive will be reunited with those who have already died. There will be an immediate reunion. Further, it is a reminder that we will be together always with our loved ones in the presence of the Lord.

CONTINUITY IN HEAVEN

1. Our earthly bodies will continue, but as glorified bodies.

2. Our distinctive personalities will continue.

3. Our memories of people and events will continue.

4. Our relationships with each other will continue.

5. Our love for each other will continue.

6. Our service will continue.

John MacArthur reminds us that verse 18 says we are to "comfort one another with these words." "The *comfort* comes from the prospect of reunion. Little comfort this would be if in the reunion we could not even recognize one another. But Paul's promise that we will all be 'together' forever implies that we shall renew fellowship with all whom we have known."[8]

OUR LOVE FOR EACH OTHER WILL CONTINUE

In heaven we will enjoy a continuity of love in a profound way. Jesus instructed us to "make friends for yourselves by means of the wealth of unrighteousness, so that when it fails, they will receive you into the eternal dwellings" (Luke 16:9). This means that people who have come to faith in Christ through our support of missions will be there to welcome us when we get to heaven. They will know who had been generous, so that they heard the gospel and went to heaven. They will be happy to see us!

Paul had a similar concept: "Who is our hope or joy or crown of exultation? Is it not even you, in the presence of our Lord Jesus at His coming?" (1 Thess. 2:19) Paul anticipated meeting in heaven those whom he had led to Christ. This means there will be knowledge of the persons and their personalities that continues in heaven. And in what way? With joy and rejoicing!

What about a family member who is already in heaven? Erwin Lutzer says, "Of course, dear widow, your husband who is in heaven continues to love you as he did on earth. Today he loves you with a fonder, sweeter, purer love. It is a love purified by God. Your child loves you; so does your mother and father. There is no more break in love than there is in continuity of thought. Death breaks ties on earth but renews them in heaven."[9]

Think of it! You will have an unending joyful relationship with your believing loved ones in heaven. Your relationship will be sweeter than it ever was on earth. And it will never end!

OUR SERVICE WILL CONTINUE

What will we do in heaven? John reminds us that "His bond-servants will serve Him" (Rev. 22:3). "Serve" (*latreusousin*) means "to worship by serving."[10] But how will we serve God? God has gifted us in this life to serve Him, and it appears that we will serve Him in a similar but expanded capacity in heaven. When we trusted Jesus Christ as our personal Savior, God endowed us with spiritual gifts (Rom. 12:6–8; 1 Cor. 12:4–11, 27–30; Eph. 4:11–12). Are our spiritual gifts employed only on this earth, or will we use them in heaven as well? Since there is a continuity of our personality, why would there not be a continuity of our giftedness? We will still be the same people that we were on the old earth; why could we not expect our giftedness to continue?

We can expect to continue to serve God in heaven with our same personality, with our same giftedness that we did on this earth. In the parable of the talents, Jesus commended the five- and two-talent men, saying, "'Well done, good and faithful slave. You were faithful with a few things, I will put you in charge of many things; enter into the joy of your master'" (Matt. 25:21, 23). Of what would the Lord put them in charge? They would continue to serve Him in concert with their abilities and giftedness. Wilbur Smith states, "There will be a number of activities in heaven which will be a continuation of our labor for Christ on earth."[11] He continues, "In heaven we will be permitted to finish many of those worthy tasks which we had dreamed to do while on earth but which neither time nor strength nor ability allowed us to achieve."[12]

Our abilities and giftedness does not end on this earth; we will continue to serve the Lord in agreement with our abilities on this earth. Lutzer expands this thought: "We will most probably continue many of the same kinds of projects we knew on earth. Artists will do art as never before; the scientist just might be invited to continue his or her exploration of God's magnificent creation. The musicians will do music; all of us will continue to learn."[13]

Randy Alcorn adds, "Because there will be continuity from the old Earth to the new, it's possible we'll continue some of the work we started on the old Earth. I believe we'll pursue some of the same things we were doing, or dreamed of doing before our death.... Others, however, may continue with work similar to what they do now whether as gardeners, engineers, builders, artists, animal trainers, musicians, scientists, craftspeople, or hundreds of other vocations."[14]

We will walk in our good works, serving Him for all eternity. Since God chose us in eternity past, that we should be holy and blameless before Him (Eph. 1:4), should we not expect the ultimate fulfillment in our walk and service for Him in eternity future? It is *reasonable* to assume that he chose us in eternity past and gifted us to serve Him for eternity future. It is *unreasonable* to assume that He chose us in eternity past to serve Him for only our threescore and ten on this old earth. He is an eternal God, and we will serve Him for all eternity.

The spiritual gifts we were given at salvation constitute who we are as believers. In continuity with who we are, we will continue to exercise our spiritual gifts. We will be serving, teaching, exhorting, giving, leading, and showing mercy according to our giftedness (Rom. 12:7–8).

* * *

There will indeed be a continuity of our lives on this old earth with our new lives on the new earth. We will see and recognize each other, hearing the familiar voices, remembering and rehearsing events from earth, enjoying each other's distinct personalities and, most of all, loving each other in greater dimension, and serving the Lord with our unique giftedness. Truly, it is heaven, where everything is *always better! It is heaven revealed!*

What Will We Do in

HEAVEN?

There are many misconceptions about our activity in heaven. The media frequently picture heaven as angelic beings playing harps while floating on a cloud. This has even affected Christians' thinking about heaven. Much thought about heaven is quite defective. And much of the teaching on prophecy has failed to develop a proper, biblical understanding of heaven.

But the Bible has a great deal to say about our activities in heaven. In fact, believers will enjoy extensive activities in the new heaven and the new earth. It will be life as God intended life to be, writes Paul Benware:

> God is going to do in the eternal state what He originally intended doing in the original creation. Mankind was created then to dwell on this earth, and that is where he will dwell in the eternal kingdom of God. This would suggest that in eternity, as in the original creation, man will be involved in various kinds of meaningful activity, learning and serving the Lord.[1]

That raises the question, What determines what we will do when heaven comes to the new earth? Will all believers have equal authority? Will our present lives, occupations, and activities determine our eternal occupation for Christ? Here are more than a dozen activities we may do in our new dwelling place.

WE WILL WORSHIP THE TRIUNE GOD

It is obvious that we will worship God in heaven, but what will that worship involve? There are scenes in the intermediate heaven that reveal the present worship in heaven. Angels, the living creatures, and elders are pictured surrounding the throne in worship with loud voices, saying, "Worthy is the Lamb that was slain to receive power and riches and wisdom and might and honor and glory and blessing" (Rev. 5:12). There will be active worship and praise of the triune God for the colossal redemption the Lord has provided for us through the blood atonement of Jesus Christ.

But worship will take on another form. What was God's original design for Adam and Eve? God commanded them to subdue the earth and "rule over . . . every living thing that moves on the earth" (Gen. 1:28). God never abrogated that command; it will be fulfilled through the rule of Jesus Christ and His servants in the eternal kingdom on earth. Every act of service will be an act of worship of God. We will be fulfilling God's original purpose for us in our service for Him—which will also constitute worship. As Randy Alcorn indicates, in this present life we are "able to be joyful, pray, and give thanks *while doing other things. . . .* we are worshiping God *as we do everything* else."[2] He adds:

> All that we do will be an act of worship. We'll enjoy full and unbroken fellowship with Christ. . . . We will overflow in gratitude and praise. We are *created* to worship God. There's no higher pleasure. At times we'll lose ourselves in praise, doing nothing but worshiping him. At other

times we'll worship him when we build a cabinet, paint a picture, cook a meal, talk with an old friend, take a walk, or throw a ball."[3]

WE WILL RULE AND ADMINISTRATE

What does it mean to rule and administrate? We can see it in its most comprehensive state with the American presidency. The American president, the chief ruler, has many administrators in finance, in education, in social work, as ambassadors to foreign countries—the list is endless. Many administer, but some have the authority to make decisions and thus rule. Ruling on the new earth will involve a wide spectrum of service for Christ.

Some believers will be actively judging, ruling, and administrating in heaven—on the new earth. In rebuking the carnal Corinthians, Paul reminded them, "Do you not know that saints will judge the world? . . . Do you not know that we will judge angels?" (1 Cor. 6:2–3a). Believers will rule with Christ, judging the world, both in the millennium and in the eternal state on the new earth (Rom. 5:17; Rev. 22:5). It is incomprehensible, but we will rule with Christ forever on the new earth (Rev. 22:5). Believers will carry out the mission and ministry of Christ through ruling and reigning on the new earth. The language is strong. "Reign" means "to rule as king."[4]

The perfect rule of Christ will pervade the earth. Justice and truth will prevail. No longer will there be terrorists blowing up planes and buildings; no longer will robberies, murders, and child abuse exist. Only the righteous will live and work on the new earth, and all will have glorified bodies—which includes new minds that focus only on truth and righteousness.

Scripture makes distinctions that determine our eternal service. The Scripture says, "If we endure, we will also reign with Him" (2 Tim. 2:12). The condition of reigning (or a particular aspect of reigning) is enduring. Paul has talked about suffering hardship for the gospel (v.

9). Those who have suffered abuse, resistance, and ridicule for the sake of the gospel will enjoy a prominent place of reigning with Christ in the eternal, unending kingdom (cf. Rom. 8:17). China, North Korea, the old Soviet Union, Muslim nations, and others have fiercely persecuted Christians. But those persecuted believers will reign and rule with Christ in His eternal kingdom.

OUR POSITIONS OF AUTHORITY WILL DIFFER

What positions of authority will we have on the new earth? What will determine our position and our rule? Christ instructed the Twelve on positions they and other believers would have on the new earth. Those who have left father, mother, brothers, sisters—who have sacrificed material possessions and left everything to follow Christ, will receive the greater reward (Matt. 19:27–30; cf. Luke 22:29–30). Jesus said, "Everyone who has left houses or brothers or sisters or father or mother or children or farms for My name's sake, will receive many times as much, and will inherit eternal life. But many who are first will be last; and the last, first" (Matt. 19:29–30). The apostles were last on the old earth but they will be first on the new earth. When Christ sits on His glorious throne—ruling—these will be first, judging the twelve tribes of Israel. But Christ promised that *everyone* who had left family and home to serve Him would be rewarded accordingly.

This should motivate believers to keep eternity in perspective. It is so easy to be caught up in the "American dream" and focus on materialism while losing the eternal blessing. Any sacrifice made in this life is entirely incidental to the enormity of the reward that believers will reap in positions of authority and service for Christ on the new earth.

In the parable of the ten minas, Jesus taught that there were differing rewards and responsibilities given for differing results in labor for Him in this life. The one who gained ten minas was set in authority over ten cities; the one who gained five minas was put in authority over five cities (Luke 19:11–19). The minas probably represent God's truth. What did His servants do with His truth? Those who are faithful in spreading God's truth will be rewarded accordingly—and it will have eternal repercussions. Those who have been faithful will have authority over cities.

What will that involve? Undoubtedly, numerous responsibilities. What is involved in ruling a city? The one ruling a city will unquestionably have subordinates overseeing differing areas of service: construction of homes (there will be homebuilding on the new earth, Isaiah 65:21), organization of education; the list is endless.

Man's original commission to rule over the earth (Gen. 1:28), which was forfeited through sin, will ultimately be fulfilled in the millennial kingdom and on the new earth for all eternity (Ps. 8:6-8). This reign will not be restricted to an era or a millennium. It will be forever on the new earth (Rev. 22:5).

WE MAY REBUILD CITIES

Picturing redeemed and restored Israel in the kingdom, the Lord declared, "They will rebuild the ruined cities and live in them" (Amos 9:14). Isaiah pictures the same event: "Then they will rebuild the ancient ruins, they will raise up the former devastations; and they will repair the ruined cities" (Isa. 61:4). This has not yet been fulfilled; this event follows the return of Christ and the establishment of His eternal kingdom on earth.

What will this involve? Pictures of the devastation in Europe following World War II revealed a destroyed continent. Yet, traveling through Europe today, there is little evidence of the war's destruction. The European countries have been rebuilt. How much more will be the renewal of the earth following Christ's return! Think of the vocations and trades that will be involved: architects, engineers, construction foremen, manufacturers, planners and designers, carpenters . . .

the list is endless. Those of us who have mastered these skills will be in our element. Those of us who have limited abilities (we hit the finger-nail instead of the metal nail) will learn quickly with keen minds and strong bodies. Those with no skills may learn anew (though not everyone will be assigned to build cities or every activity shown here).

WE MAY BUILD HOMES

I have several architect friends. What will they be doing on the new earth? There will be a continuity between their work on this earth and their work in heaven on the new earth. Carson designs church buildings on this earth; he will design buildings for the glory of God, whether there will be buildings of worship or not. Bill has also designed commercial and residential buildings throughout his life. On the new earth he will carry on his abilities and continue to design buildings.

As a young man I worked as an architectural draftsman, designing homes. I took enormous pleasure in driving by a home that I had designed and was later built and occupied. Isaiah speaks of a future day, which relates to both the millennium and the new earth in eternity, when "they will build houses and inhabit them" (Isa. 65:21). But the believers will enjoy life on the new earth in an entirely new measure. Locks on doors will be unnecessary. Police cruisers will be non-existent. There will be peace and security in that future day: "Then my people will live in a peaceful habitation, and in secure dwellings and in undisturbed resting places" (Isa. 32:18). Police sirens will not be heard. There will be no threat of burglary or assault. Peace will reign in Messiah's rule on the new earth.

With the construction of new houses, there is also the reminder that many auxiliary professions and occupations will exist. House construction calls for many trades; in today's world we would think of architects, lumber dealers, electricians, plumbers, roofers, and many others. How many of these will apply to the new earth is indeterminable. But likely there will be more activity than we can imagine.

SOME WILL COMPOSE AND WRITE MUSIC

George Frederick Handel has blessed the Christian world through his musical composition of the *Messiah*. It is truly a musical masterpiece that glorifies God and exalts the Savior. Is it not possible that Handel will continue to compose music that glorifies God? The Scriptures remind us concerning those who have died that "their deeds follow with them" (Rev. 14:13). Not only do believers go to heaven, but their works "follow with them." "With" (*meta*) suggests that the works follow "in close association with"[5] the believer. The works go to glory together with the believer.

Music will constitute an important aspect of the environment of heaven. There will be musical instruments (Rev. 5:8; 14:2; 15:2) and singing (Rev. 5:9). If there are musical instruments in praise of God on this earth (1 Chron. 16:5–6; Neh. 12:27), why not on the new earth?

Imagine the wonderful music that will continue to honor and exalt the Lord. Classical composers who know the Lord, perhaps Johann Sebastian Bach and Franz Joseph Haydn, will have much to contribute to heaven's music. But so will more recent composers like Fanny Crosby, Horatio Spafford, and William Cowper, and even more recent composers like John W. Peterson, Bill Gaither, and Steven Curtis Chapman. And some lesser-known writers and composers of Christ-honoring music will blossom with minds and talents no longer dulled by fatigue, distraction, or other limitations. Think of wonderful lyricists and composers continuing to create music throughout eternity for God's people to sing and praise the Lord! What a wonderful time that will be!

SOME WILL PLAY MUSICAL INSTRUMENTS

Probably most people have attempted to play some musical instrument. I took piano lessons when I was a young boy, but one day the piano teacher told my mother, "Save your thirty-five cents" (which was the cost of a half-hour lesson in those days). So I stopped the piano lessons. But after Helen's homegoing, I bought a piano, and more than fifty years after I stopped taking lessons, I have begun plunking on the piano again. Perhaps I'll play the piano in heaven. Will there be pianos in heaven? Why not? There will be trumpets and other instruments; why not pianos?

As Alcorn has noted, we will not start over on the new earth. There will be a continuity with the knowledge, abilities, and progress from the old earth—whatever honors the Lord.[6] So, many of us who didn't do as well on the piano, clarinet, trumpet, and violin will have an eternity of opportunity to develop skill playing an instrument that we never developed a talent for on the old earth.

WE WILL SERVE

The tribulation martyrs are pictured in heaven, where "they are before the throne of God; and they serve Him day and night in His temple" (Rev. 7:15). In this passage "serve" carries the sense of adoration.[7] It has a similar sense in Revelation 22:3, where "His bond-servants will serve Him" in heaven. In other references it is used for praise and prayer and "will include every form of divine worship."[8] We may then understand that the redeemed will serve the Lord in many different ways in glory, all of which involve worship, praise, and adoration.

Our finite minds are stymied when conceiving the varied ways we will serve the Lord. We serve Him in diverse ways on this earth; we will serve Him in diverse ways in heaven—undoubtedly, more diverse and more profound ways than now.

Paul's letter to Titus may evoke a similar thought. Since Christ has redeemed and purified us as a special people for Himself, should we not expect to zealously serve Him for all eternity (Titus 2:14)?

WHAT WILL WE DO?

1. We will worship the triune God.

2. We will rule and administrate.

3. We will have different positions of authority.

4. We may rebuild cities.

5. We may build homes.

6. Some will compose and write music.

7. Some will play musical instruments.

8. We will serve.

9. Some will farm.

10. Some will cultivate orchards.

11. Some will raise livestock.

12. We may fish . . . if we want to.

13. We will be totally fulfilled.

SOME WILL FARM

My father-in-law, who was a grain farmer for forty years, had high moral principles and a strong trust in God. Although he farmed in Manitoba, north of North Dakota, where the grain-growing season is short and frost can come as late as May and begin as early as September, he never farmed on Sunday. It was the Lord's Day. If he didn't get his crop off the field because of frost or rain, he simply accepted it from the Lord.

In this life farmers are plagued with problems. Both drought and torrential rain can destroy crops, as can hail and disease. On the new earth, some of us will farm—and we will be very successful. We will always have bumper crops, yielding bushels per acre no farmer on the old earth ever saw. Isaiah promises, "He will give you rain for the seed which you will sow in the ground, and bread from the yield of the ground, and it will be rich and plenteous" (Isa. 30:23). The Lord will give the right amount of rain and sunshine to produce a rich harvest with each sowing.

On the new earth, a farmer will never fear failure! God Himself will sow the crops, and the earth will respond to its master, producing abundant crops (Hos. 2:22). Each crop will evidence God's blessing since God promises, "How blessed will you be, you who sow beside all waters" (Isa. 32:20). Farmers will have no need for crop insurance on the new earth!

Amos pictures those days on the new earth: "When the plowman will overtake the reaper and the treader of grapes him who sows seed; when the mountains will drip sweet wine and all the hills will be dissolved" (Amos 9:13). The crops will be so enormous that the harvesting will take so long, the one planting the new crop will overtake the one threshing.

SOME WILL CULTIVATE ORCHARDS

Isaiah prophesied, "They will also plant vineyards and eat their fruit" on the new earth (Isa. 65:21b). This promise entails several things. No one else will eat the fruit—no marauders, no enemies, no insects—just us and those we give it to. In a perfect world, there will be perfect vineyards—lush, beautiful, productive (Amos 9:13-14). There will be no weeds to contend with on the new earth (Isa. 55:13).

It is reasonable to conclude that if there will be vineyards on the new earth, there will be numerous other fruitful groves. In fact, we can expect that every kind of tree God created will be there.

SOME WILL RAISE LIVESTOCK

Will there be cattle on the new earth? Why not? God didn't create the world and all it contains to be destroyed after only a few millennia. He created the world to be enjoyed and ruled over by man. That was His purpose from the beginning, and that will be fulfilled on the new earth for all eternity (Ps. 8:3-9).

Cattle—large herds of cattle—have been an integral part of American history and the opening of the West when large herds grazed on the prairies. But with the burgeoning cities, that scene is uncommon today. Isaiah looks to the future when in the millennium and on the new earth there will be large herds of cattle: "On that day your livestock will graze in a roomy pasture" (Isa. 30:23b). Cows giving milk will be prolific (Joel 3:18).

On the new earth believers will live in peaceful security, enjoying placid country scenes, with oxen and donkeys and other animals freely roaming the countryside (Isa. 32:20). Imagine the deer, elk, moose, bears, wolves, coyotes, camels, elephants—all the species on the earth —friendly and docile! We will be able to pet animals that are inherently wild today. They will be docile tomorrow.

WE MAY FISH . . . IF WE WANT TO

Undoubtedly, many men will look forward to this. In the millennial kingdom there will be fishing in abundance: "And it will come about that fishermen will stand beside it; from Engedi to Eneglaim there will be a place for the spreading of nets. Their fish will be according to their kinds, like the fish of the Great Sea, very many" (Ezek. 47:10). Since there is a continuity between the millennial kingdom and the new heaven and new earth, it is reasonable to expect fishing to continue in the eternal state. While there will be no sea, we know there will be a river (Rev. 22:1) and apparently there is a connection between the river mentioned in Ezekiel 47:1 and Revelation 22:1.

If you're now a poor fisherman or woman, take heart! You won't prick your finger or draw blood hooking the bait, and the fish will be abundant, so you won't need to locate the perfect spot. If you never learned on earth to fish and were a poor angler, this may be a great opportunity to take up this sport. The fish, so many in number, will almost help you learn as they teem in the lakes, rivers, and streams,

WE WILL BE TOTALLY FULFILLED

We can conclude that there will be innumerable things we will do in heaven. The work and worship we began for Christ on earth will continue in heaven, on the new earth. Many acknowledge the continuity. Herbert Wolf says, "Some of the features of Isaiah's description of the messianic age [Isaiah 65:20–25] seem to look ahead to the eternal state."[9] Randy Alcorn concludes, "We'll be a great community on the New Earth. The gifts, skills, passions, and tasks God grants each of us will not only be for his glory and our good but also for the good of our larger family. God will rejoice as we thrive together, interdependently, in the New Earth's continuously creative culture."[10]

We will be totally fulfilled, working, serving God—and fully enjoying every moment. It is heaven, where everything is *always better*, in every way! *It is heaven revealed!*

What Will Our RELATIONSHIPS with OTHERS Be Like?

A teary-eyed lady asked me emphatically, "I want to know what my relationship with my husband will be like in heaven! Why can't we be married in heaven?" She was upset because she and her husband have a wonderful marriage. Their love for each other is evident. Her question is valid. What *will* our relationship with our loved ones be like? Will we know each other? Will our relationship be *less* in heaven than on earth? What will we remember of our life together on earth?

The Scripture has more to say on these issues than most people realize. But in addition to studying the pertinent Scriptures, an underlying understanding must be kept in mind. This is earth; our future lies in heaven. Heaven is *always better* than earth—in every dimension. There is *no realm* in which earth is better. In no way will we ever be poorer in heaven than on earth.

Everything will be better in heaven. That is an underlying principle that we must continually bear in mind. Do you have a good relationship on earth with your spouse? It will be *better* in heaven. Are we surrounded by a lot of love on earth? We will experience *more* love in heaven.

WE WILL RETAIN OUR IDENTITIES

Scripture makes it abundantly clear that we—in continuity with our earthly life—will retain our distinctive identities. We will be ourselves—although glorified—and not someone else.

Many Scriptures emphasize this important truth. In describing our glorification, Paul uses the term "we" continuously: "Behold, I tell you a mystery, *we* will not all sleep, but *we* will all be changed, in a moment, in the twinkling of an eye, at the last trumpet; for the trumpet will sound, and the dead will be raised imperishable, and *we* will all be changed" (1 Cor. 15:51–52; emphasis added).

Scripture's consistent use of "we" indicates the continuity of our identities in heaven. "We can therefore conclude with conviction that life in the heavenly world will preserve personal identity. There will be continuity of our personhood. . . . the self with which we were endowed by the Creator in His gift of life to us . . . *that self* will endure into eternity. We ourselves, and not another, are destined to behold the face of God and share in the life of heaven. Death cannot destroy us. Our personhood is immortal. By God's faithful grace we shall endure eternally."[1]

WE WILL BE REUNITED WITH OUR FAMILIES

Do the Scriptures give us any information that there will be reunion with loved ones, that in heaven we will know and enjoy the ones we loved on earth? Indeed, there are a number of Scripture passages that clearly tell us of glorious reunion with our loved ones!

When Abraham died, the Bible says, "Abraham breathed his last . . . and he was gathered to his people" (Gen. 25:8). Similarly, when Isaac died, the Bible declares, "Isaac breathed his last and died and was gathered to his people" (Gen. 35:29). And of Jacob it also states, "When Jacob finished charging his sons, he drew his feet into the bed and breathed his last, and was gathered to his people" (Gen. 49:33). What does it mean that he was "gathered to his people"? It means Abraham was reunited with Sarah and with his family in heaven. It means Isaac was reunited with Rebekah and with his family in heaven. It means Jacob was reunited with Rachel as well as with his parents and grandparents.

Should we think that God would give us a wonderful, loving relationship with family and friends for forty or fifty years, only to be terminated, never to be enjoyed again? *Impossible!*

A New England woman, Mary Cabot, mourned the death of her brother, Roy, in the Civil War. She found no comfort in the Puritan doctrine that implied she would not have a familiar relationship with him after death. Her aunt, Winifred Forceythe, criticized the Puritans allegorizing the book of Revelation, saying it should be interpreted literally. Hence, she wrote:

"[Eternity] cannot be the great blank ocean which most of us have somehow or other been brought up to feel that it is, which will swallow up, in a pitiless glorified way, all the little brooks of our delight. So I expect to have my beautiful home, and my husband, and [my daughter] Faith, as I had them here; with many differences, and great ones, but *mine* just the same."[2]

Think of your family get-togethers. The big meals. The visiting. The fellowship. When our sons and their families would come home, Helen liked to fix roast duck with many trimmings. She would prepare an enormous feast that we all looked forward to. Good eating and good fellowship. It was always a great time. In heaven we will be reunited with our loved ones, and we will have greater get-togethers than we ever had on earth. *It is heaven!*

I recently returned from visiting my friend from grade school

John Derksen. He and his wife, Hedie, took me to a Mennonite Central Committee gathering in Winnipeg where hundreds of people had come together. As we walked along, John kept introducing me to different people, among whom was Bill Schroeder. That was interesting since my mother's maiden name is Schroeder. Bill Schroeder is an historian who wrote *Mennonite Historical Atlas*. I was especially interested in talking to him since I was planning a trip in the fall to Berlin, where I would be teaching. Then I planned to go further into northeastern Germany and the Gdansk area of Poland, which was formerly Germany, to locate precisely where my and my wife's ancestors lived in the 1500s.

So I asked Bill Schroeder, "Do you know the village where the Schroeders lived in the 1500s?"

"Absolutely," he responded—and he gave me the name of the village! Then in October my son Terry and I had the intense joy of visiting the towns in historic Germany where both my ancestors and my wife's ancestors lived in the 1500s.

Here on this old, fallen earth we try to discover our ancestry—and that is worthwhile and exciting. But imagine meeting your relatives in heaven! I won't have to search to find my believing ancestors from the 1500s and beyond. Imagine the discussions you will have with your relatives. Each one rehearsing their history and life on this earth—and we will have time—limitless time!

The recurring phrase in Scripture, "He was gathered to his people," is a clear biblical statement affirming the reunion of loved ones in heaven. But there is more biblical evidence. When David's son from Bathsheba died, David went into the temple and worshiped; then he said, "I will go to him, but he will not return to me" (2 Sam. 12:23). David understood that when he died, he would be reunited in heaven with his infant son.

When the apostle Paul comforted the grieving Thessalonians concerning those who had died, he reminded them, "The dead in Christ will rise first, then we who are alive and remain will be caught up together with them in the clouds to meet the Lord in the air, and so *we* shall always be with the Lord" (1 Thess. 4:16b–17).

In the greatest hour of grief, the temporary separation of loved ones through death, Scripture provides a glorious promise of comfort. Believers have a genuine, unfailing hope of a future reunion with loved ones. Beyond comfort, we can find joy in anticipating our future reunion. Of Jesus' first meeting with His disciples after His resurrection, Matthew wrote simply, "Jesus met them and greeted them" (Matt. 28:9). But the original text reflects a strong, exclamatory statement. "Greeted" stands last in the Greek text, adding emphasis. Jesus actually said, "Greetings! Rejoice! Be glad!" All of these words apply.[3] The word "greeted" can be used as a synonym for another Greek word meaning "to rejoice exuberantly" (cf. Rev. 19:7).[4]

When the disciples heard and saw Jesus, they "took hold of His feet" (Matt. 28:9). The language reflects the emotion of the moment. Recognizing it was Jesus, in their excitement they seized His feet.[5] In our reunion with our loved ones, there will be enormous excitement— followed by our embracing! We will be overwhelmed with joy at seeing our loved ones—husband, wife, father, mother, son, daughter—and we will grasp them and hug them with the most loving embrace we have ever experienced!

Yes, it is true, and yes, it is coming. This should encourage us to keep focused on the future while we continue faithfully in the present (Col. 3:1-4). We will rejoice exuberantly when we meet our loved ones in glory. What a glorious day that will be!

WE WILL KNOW EACH OTHER EVEN BETTER

When Jesus was transfigured on the mountain and Moses and Elijah appeared, Peter and the apostles recognized Moses and Elijah (Matt.

17:3). It means there is an identification with the past. We will recognize one another. There is a continuity with the past. The bodies we had on the old earth will be recognizable in heaven. The ones we loved in those special bodies on earth will be the ones that we will see, know, and love in even greater dimension in heaven.

In the story of the rich man and Lazarus, the rich man remembered his life on earth (Luke 16:27–28). He remembered his father's home. He remembered his brothers. He remembered their spiritual need. He remembered his home and the situation in his home. He remembered Lazarus. If those in hell have this knowledge and remembrance of their earthly lives, it is surely true of those in heaven. As the rich man remembered details of his family life, so we too, in heaven, will remember both the people in our lives and the details of our lives on earth.

J. Oswald Sanders says, "Life in heaven will bring enrichment, not impoverishment.... George MacDonald once posed the wry question, 'Shall we be greater fools in Paradise than we are here?'"[6] We will not have less knowledge in heaven; we will have more knowledge. If we know each other well here, we will know each other better in heaven.

There will be a glorious, happy reunion of loved ones—family and close friends—in heaven. Never to be separated! And we will know each other *better* than we knew each other on earth.

We will also be able to recall the events of our life on earth. Think of some of the memorable events that are fixed in your mind, that bring you great joy as you reflect on them. A family trip you took together, a special event where you ate together and had great fellowship ... You'll remember them all and more. Things that you have forgotten here will be remembered and discussed in heaven. What a joyous time of fellowship that will be!

But even more than that, you will know people you have never met before. You will have fellowship with extended family members who were believers in Christ. Abraham will be banqueting with Isaac and Jacob—his son and grandson—in the kingdom (Matt. 8:11; Luke 13:28). You will enjoy getting to know family members whom you have never seen. As fellow believers in Christ, you and I will dine together in Christ's kingdom!

I've done some research on family history and am able to trace my ancestry on both sides specifically to the early 1700s and generally to the 1500s. Of the ancestors who are known, we have not discovered an unbeliever among them. This is very encouraging. On that reunion day we will recognize and talk (excitedly, no doubt) to our great grandparents and great-great-great grandparents. Beyond that we will recognize biblical characters. I suspect the apostle Paul will have many people converging on him to talk with him. But we will have an eternity to fellowship with our newly discovered family and friends!

WE WILL REMEMBER ONE ANOTHER MORE FULLY

From the moment we reach heaven, we will not only know one another, but we will know each other fully, perfectly. "For now we see in a mirror dimly, but then face to face; now I know in part, but then I will know fully just as I also have been fully known" (1 Cor. 13:12).

Erwin Lutzer says, "In heaven, we will know just like we do on earth, except more so."[7] Our knowledge of one another is incomplete on earth; it is limited because our minds are limited. But in heaven we will have expanded knowledge, a fuller knowledge of one another. Of course, this does not mean we will know everything; we will not. Only God is omniscient (Ps. 139:1–6); we will not know everything that God knows. But we will have a fuller, clearer knowledge of each other because our minds will be unsullied by sin. We will not misinterpret words or motives; we will understand one another precisely.

The Scripture reminds us, "Beloved, now we are children of God, and it has not appeared as yet what we will be. We know that when He appears, we will be like Him, because we will see Him just as He is" (1 John 3:2). This encouraging Scripture reminds us that we will see one another in perfection, not with faulty knowledge or understanding. We will see Jesus exactly as He is; we will see each other exactly as we are.

James Montgomery Boice said, "We will see each other not as we are now or have been but as we are meant to be."[8] What a glorious thought! All our warts and wrinkles will be gone. We will see one another in perfection! The one you love so much on earth will be even lovelier and more wonderful in heaven. That is truly an incomprehensible thought!

I recall both the morning and evening of January 30, 2005. After I had parked our car, my wife and I walked to the church building, holding hands as we always did. I distinctly recall the emotion that overwhelmed me. I was thrilled to hold her hand; I felt like a newly engaged young man, head over heels in love and excited to be walking hand-in-hand with my beloved. She thrilled me as much on that day as the first day forty-five years earlier. Some eighteen hours after that evening hand-in-hand walk to church, Helen was in heaven.

When we meet in heaven, Helen and I will be perfect, and I will love her even more than I did on earth; she will thrill me even more than in this fallen state. It is heaven! Our relationship, our love will be even greater!

WE WILL HAVE FELLOWSHIP

Our good friends Zenon and Sue enjoyed coming to our home to fellowship with us over a meal. When Zenon knew they were coming, he would fast for the entire day. He knew the kind of meal that was waiting for him at our house! Helen loved to prepare a sumptuous meal for our guests. More than once I told her she had the gift of hospitality. And she used it. She would normally fix several main meat dishes and numerous side dishes of exotic fruit and vegetables, plus an enormous dessert.

OUR RELATIONSHIPS WITH OTHERS

1. We will retain our identities.

2. We will be reunited with our families.

3. We will know each other even better.

4. We will remember one another more fully.

5. We will have fellowship.

6. We will love each other in a greater dimension.

7. We will not remember the bad things.

8. We will retain our ethnic identities.

9. We will have perfect physical features.

We had wonderful, relaxing fellowship with our friends in our home. They would tell us we had a peaceful home; there was a peaceful spirit in our home.

After Helen's homegoing, our son Jeremy found a menu that she had planned to fix for the family for her birthday, only two days later. Jeremy and his family were coming for dinner, and Helen was preparing a special meal. And along with the meal we had anticipated fellowship. We often dined European style—*Gemuetlichkeit*—we weren't rushed, we didn't hurry, we sat for long hours, visiting with each other and enjoying one another's company at the dinner table.

That is a small foretaste of the glorious fellowship we will have in heaven! Isaiah pictures this grandiose scene: "The Lord of hosts will prepare a lavish banquet for all peoples on this mountain; a banquet of aged wine, choice pieces with marrow, and refined, aged wine" (Isa. 25:6). The celebration of Messiah's kingdom rule on earth will involve wonderful fellowship, illustrated by a banquet scene. The description involves "the choice luxuries of an Eastern banquet."[9]

Jesus similarly describes the fellowship of believers in the kingdom of heaven: "Many will come from east and west, and recline at the table with Abraham, Isaac and Jacob in the kingdom of heaven" (Matt. 8:11; cf. Luke 13:29). Abraham, Isaac, and Jacob were family. These passages remind us again that there will be family reunion and fellowship in heaven, eating together, enjoying each other's company.

Jonathan Edwards suggested the Lord's Supper on this earth was a foretaste of the ineffably sublime heavenly communion we will enjoy. A major measure of our joy in heaven will be the recognition of our friends from earth and the perfect, fulfilling fellowship we will have in heaven.[10] Friendships begun on earth do not terminate at death. They will continue in a far more fulfilling realization in heaven. Wrong thoughts, faulty motives, suspicions—they will all be absent in heaven. Fellowship will be cemented by a pure love flowing from everyone.

Jesus depicted the joyous fellowship of like-minded believers over a sumptuous meal. One of the many joys of the millennial kingdom and the eternal state will be the endless discussion and genuine fellowship with one another.

In our fast-paced life in the western world in the twenty-first century there is a neglect of fellowship. We rush through the day and at night get captivated by television or technology and fail to enjoy the peaceful discussion that fosters fellowship. Because of television, the Internet, and other technology, the average American family spends a scant seven minutes a day all together. In that future day, we will be fulfilled in every element, including fellowship with our loved ones and also with many we have never met before.

WE WILL LOVE EACH OTHER
IN A GREATER DIMENSION

On this earth we have enjoyed a love relationship in our marriages and in our homes. The love we enjoy in marriage and family is a great gift from God. But what will it be in heaven? Will this continue? Will we have a unique love relationship with the people we loved on earth?

The Scripture says when Sarah died, "Abraham went in to mourn for Sarah and to weep for her" (Gen. 23:2b). Abraham loved Sarah intensely. Scripture also says that Abraham was an alien on the old earth; he was looking for a permanent city with foundations—a city that was lasting (Heb. 11:10). The context of Hebrews 11:8–12 is about Abraham and Sarah. Within that context it says Abraham was looking for a city of God. Without Sarah? Surely not. He was looking for a better city, a better country, together with Sarah and the people he loved.

If Abraham loved his wife in a fallen, sinful earth, would he love her more or less in a "better country"? Clearly, Abraham will love Sarah more in the new heaven and the new earth. Every redeemed believer will have a *better* love relationship in heaven than on this old earth—no matter how wonderful it was on this earth. And there will be a continuing love relationship on the new earth because it is earth—there is a continuity with the old earth. The new earth will be renovated, restored, and purified—and the new home for love relationships will be beyond what we can imagine on this old earth.

John MacArthur says, "I love my wife. She's my best friend and my dearest companion in every area of life. If those are your thoughts about your spouse as well, don't despair! You will enjoy an eternal companionship in heaven that is more perfect than any earthly partnership."[11] There will be renewed love and greater love in the "better country."

WE WILL NOT REMEMBER THE BAD THINGS

All of us have spoken words we would like to retract. How much hurt has been inflicted through harsh words; how much harm has been done through rudeness and even physical hurt. Will those things be remembered in heaven? Randy Alcorn suggests:

> We'll be capable of choosing not to recall or dwell on anything that would diminish Heaven's joy. . . . The comfort [for enduring bad things] implies memory of what happened. If we had no memory of the bad things why should we need comfort? . . . Our minds will be clearer in Heaven, not foggier. Memory is basic to personality. The law of continuity requires that we will remember our past lives.[12]

While the martyred believers remembered that they had been killed for their faith (Rev. 6:9–11), it is uncertain whether this means believers will remember all the bad things. Scripture is clear that there will be nothing that causes sorrow or sadness (Rev. 21:4). If the memory of evil events would cause sadness in heaven, then those things will not be remembered.

The Lord says, "For behold, I create new heavens and a new earth; and the former things shall not be remembered or to mind" (Isa. 65:17). Forgetting the bad things of life is linked to the creation of the new heavens and the new earth. In that new environment the hurtful things of this life will be erased. The difficulties with family members who are also believers will be forgotten. We will be able to have fellowship with other believers with whom we had problems on earth. Life in the new heaven and the new earth necessitates forgetting the sorrowful things of this life.

WE WILL RETAIN OUR ETHNIC IDENTITIES

Ethnicity will also continue into the new heaven and new earth. Worshiping the Lord in the New Jerusalem are the nations (*ethne*), the redeemed ethnic groups on the earth. The different, distinct ethnic people will continue in heaven. As noted in chapter 9, we will recognize each other, and part of that recognizing will be our ethnic features (in youthful, ageless bodies, of course; see pages 131–32).

In investigating our ancestral backgrounds, Helen and I have discovered that our ancestors lived only some ten miles apart from one another five hundred years ago, heralding from small villages in the vicinity of Elbing, in northeastern Germany in the 1500s. (I had the privilege of locating those villages and visiting them this summer. It was an emotional time.) We will retain our ethnicity. I suspect I will continue to speak high German to my parents and the low German, Dutch dialect to my mother-in-law and father-in-law (and English to Helen!).

Isaiah saw that glorious, future day when Messiah's kingdom would be inaugurated and when the glorious millennial kingdom would give rise to the eternal state of the new heaven and the new earth. In that day "nations will stream" to Jerusalem, which will be elevated to reflect its preeminent righteous rule in the world (Isa. 2:2–3). The nations ("*Goyim*") reflect the diverse ethnic groups that will continue in the millennium and in the eternal state.

"It is an error, however, to assume that national identity will be lost in eternity," wrote Bible scholar and seminary president John Walvoord. "Just as there will be individual identity, so also there will be racial identity, and individuals will inevitably carry throughout eternity an identification related to some extent to their place in the history of the world. . . . national identity seems a natural corollary to individual identity."[13] Gordon Lewis and Bruce Demarest add, "As distinct, recognizable persons, we will retain our *gender and ethnic characteristics.*"[14]

So on the new earth there will be distinctly individual Americans, Jews, Germans, French, Russians, Chinese, Indians—redeemed people who retain their individual and ethnic distinctions for eternity.

Some may not discover their ethnicities until they get to heaven! While in seminary I asked a fellow seminarian if he knew what his name meant. He replied that he did not. I explained that he had a wonderful name; his name meant "happy disposition." He had a German name but didn't seem to be aware of it.

Gentiles who are redeemed and converted and love the name of the Lord will be privileged to join the redeemed Hebrew people in worshiping the Lord in Jerusalem during the millennium (Isa. 56:6-8; 60:13; Rev. 21:24). In that future day the light of Christ will be both the truth about Christ and also the brilliant glory that will illuminate the entire world. The nations of the world will be in awe of the resplendent glory of God that fills the earth (Isa. 66:18). The Hebrew believers will fulfill their original purpose in declaring God's glory to the Gentile nations (Isa. 66:19).

For all eternity, in the new heaven and the new earth, all humanity —Jews and Gentiles, redeemed believers from diverse ethnicity— will worship the Lord (Isa. 66:22–23). And the Lord will dwell in their midst (Zech. 2:11).

Truth will emanate from Jerusalem, attracting Gentiles to the exalted city (Mic. 4:1–2). For all eternity, believers will continue to learn and grow in the knowledge of the Lord.

WE WILL HAVE PERFECT PHYSICAL FEATURES

Some of you may ask, "But will I still be so short, or so skinny, or overweight, or bald?" No, we will be identifiable but perfect in every way. The family members whom you love, who have gone on ahead, you will recognize, only they will be better in every way. And so will you and I.

John MacArthur reminds us, "We will forever be who we are now— only without any of our faults or infirmities."[15] Think of it. Each of us and our loved ones will be all that we have known them (and us) to be but without physical or spiritual defects. We won't complain about our appearance; we will be perfect in every way, yet distinct and recognizable according to our earthly appearance. And we will be satisfied.

BETTER THAN EVER

What a phenomenal encouragement it is to remind ourselves that our relationships with our believing loved ones will continue in heaven— better than ever! Death has brought only a temporary separation. Whether alone for five or twenty years, it is only a brief moment by eternity's time. Then an eternal reunion with our loved ones will be ushered in. Our tears will be gone, and there will be endless smiles, joyous reunion, perfect fellowship, and endless love.

Oh, the anticipation of that glorious day! It is heaven—where it is *always better!* It is heaven revealed.

13

What Will Our RELATIONSHIP with GOD Be Like?

The Old Testament reports that though they were chosen by God, the people of Israel could not approach God physically. God's presence was a frightening phenomenon, evidenced by thunder, lightning, and a thick cloud (Exod. 19:16). If the people attempted to approach God, they would be judged with death (Exod. 19:21). Moses was prohibited from seeing God, who warned him, "You cannot see My face, for no man can see Me and live!" (Exod. 33:20).

When Isaiah saw the Lord, sitting on His throne, he became frightened, saying, "Woe is me, for I am ruined! ... For my eyes have seen the king, the Lord of hosts" (Isa. 6:5).

And long before Moses and Isaiah, Job exhibited enormous faith when he exclaimed, "Even after my skin is destroyed, yet from my flesh I shall see God, whom I myself shall behold, and whom my eyes shall see and not another" (Job 19:26-27). But he would not see the Lord in his earthly life; Job was looking ahead to a distant day.

"No man can see me and live," God has declared.

WE WILL SEE—AND KNOW—HIM

But a time will come when all who believe in Him will see Him. In heaven we will enjoy a unique fellowship that would have been thought utterly impossible. Jesus promises, "Blessed are the pure in heart, for they shall see God" (Matt. 5:8). But this involves more than visual sight. In seeing God, we will *know* God.[1]

This is beyond our comprehension—to see God and to know God! This will result in a satisfaction that on this present earth is incomprehensible: seeing Him and living in His presence (Ps. 11:7; 140:13). David anticipated that day, "As for me, I shall behold Your face in righteousness; I will be satisfied with Your likeness when I awake" (Ps. 17:15). Satisfied! On this present earth we are never fully satisfied. Momentary satisfaction may come from material things—acquisition of a new car, a new home—or there may be momentary satisfaction in fellowship with friends. But it is never lasting, never permanent. On that day we will be *fully and permanently satisfied!*

First John 3:2 promises, "Beloved, now we are children of God, and it has not appeared as yet what we will be. We know that when He appears, we will be like Him, because we will see Him just as He is." On that glorious day we will have transformed bodies—resurrection bodies like the body of Christ. Moreover, we will be transformed spiritually as well; our mind, heart, and will then shall reflect only spiritual vitality. In that realm, "we will see Him."

This sinful body and mortal nature cannot appreciate the magnitude of Christ's glory—but in our resurrection bodies we will look on Him and "see Him just as He is." We will see God the Son with wondrous appreciation and love, with joy and gladness at being made in His image. And we will behold the glory of God the Father as well.

Surely this is one of the most profound statements in Scripture: "We shall see Him just as He is." How shall we understand this? B. F. Westcott offers two possibilities, not entirely divergent:

We shall see God, and therefore, since this is possible, we must be like Him; or, We shall see God, and in that Presence we shall reflect His glory and be transformed into His likeness. Both thoughts are scriptural; and perhaps the two thoughts are not very sharply distinguished here.[2]

John promised, "They will see His face, and His name will be on their foreheads" (Rev. 22:4). When John spoke of seeing God's face, his was an anthropomorphic statement, since God does not have a physical form. To see His face would suggest seeing the essence of God, just as seeing His back would imply seeing the outshining or the effect of God without seeing His essence (Exod. 33:23). But seeing God would also involve seeing Jesus, the second person of the Trinity.[3] Jesus is eternally the God-Man, having both a physical, glorified human body but equally being deity.

WE WILL BE LIKE CHRIST

"We will be like Him." That staggering statement in 1 John 3:2 is almost incomprehensible. We read the Gospels with wonder and amazement as we see the uniqueness of Jesus Christ—the words He spoke, the miracles He performed. Will we be like that? Will we be able to do the things Jesus did? No. Jesus alone remains the second person of the Trinity. He alone is forever the God-Man, the theanthropic person.

The emphasis on being like Him is emphatic; the word "like" (Greek "*Homoioi*") stands in the emphatic position in the Greek text. What does it mean? "This likeness of man redeemed and perfected to God is the likeness of the creature reflecting the glory of the Creator."[4] In our glorified, sinless bodies we will reflect the glory of the Lord, but we will not be deity.

This is the final stage in our salvation. God predestined and called us in eternity past; He justified us in history when we trusted in Christ; He will glorify us in the future on that great resurrection day (1 Thess.

4:16–17; 1 Cor. 15:52–53). On that great day we will receive powerful, imperishable bodies (1 Cor. 15:42–43). We will reflect the glory of God in those transformed bodies. They will be perfect, sinless, imperishable bodies—in that sense we will be like Him. "Then the transfiguration of Christians will enable them to see the transfigured Christ as He is," Schneider writes.[5] On that day we will be fulfilled in our relationship with Jesus Christ. In our sinless, glorified bodies we will see Christ with new eyes; we will see Him in all His magnificence as the glorified God-Man and Sovereign King of the universe.

WE WILL FELLOWSHIP WITH CHRIST

Undoubtedly, when we read the Gospels telling us how the disciples walked, lived, ate, and journeyed with Jesus for three years, we wonder what a blessing it must have been for the Twelve. To hear Jesus teach, to see Him heal the sick, to feel His compassion—clearly, they were privileged. But a day is coming when we will equally enjoy fellowship with the Lord Jesus!

We are promised that in heaven "the tabernacle of God is among men, and He will dwell among them, and they shall be His people, and God Himself will be among them" (Rev. 21:3). The term "tabernacle" is a reminder of God's fellowship with the Israelites in the wilderness; it was the reminder of His presence in their midst. As they moved in the desert, God was always present with them, evidenced by the tabernacle. Here it means the "abiding presence of God."[6]

In heaven God will tabernacle with His people in a new way: He will dwell "among" His redeemed people (Rev. 21:3). The word *among* (Gk. *meta*) occurs three times in this verse and beautifully illustrates the relationship of God with His people. *Meta* is a preposition emphasizing being in company with someone, of being in a close relationship as Jesus was with His disciples on earth (cf. Matt. 26:69, 71; Mark

Our New Relationship with God

1. We will see—and know—Him.
2. We will be like Christ.
3. We will fellowship with Christ.
4. We will have close association with Christ.
5. We will worship Him.
6. We will marvel at His glory.

3:14).[7] In heaven we will be in close fellowship, in close association with the Lord Himself.

I think back to our early married years, when in our Mennonite culture, fellowship was a very important element. Sunday afternoons were always spent in fellowship with others. We would visit other couples unannounced—that was common. You didn't normally call to let them know you were coming; you just showed up! And visited. Around four o'clock the ladies prepared *faspa*, a distinctly Mennonite meal of cold cuts and sweets—very suitable for continued fellowship. It was a great time for talking, visiting with friends. Imagine how much more wonderful our fellowship will be in heaven with God Himself and with other believers!

What was the fellowship of Jesus with the disciples? There was discussion, but more important, He was talking and they were listening—and learning. Undoubtedly, our fellowship with the Lord will involve Him teaching us, and we will learn. And the learning process will continue, for all eternity. We will never arrive, and so the fellowship will never diminish or end; it will continue forever.

WE WILL HAVE CLOSE ASSOCIATION WITH CHRIST

During my married years, I always enjoyed just being with Helen, whether talking with her or even being quiet. We frequently drove to Cypress Gardens, about a two-hour drive from our home. While I enjoyed seeing the beauty of Cypress Gardens, I enjoyed the drive there just as much, knowing Helen was sitting beside me, fellowshiping along the way.

Shortly after Helen's homegoing, I read John 17:24, and the verse jolted me. I have meditated on the verse several times since. Jesus prays, "Father, I desire that they also, whom You have given Me, be with Me where I am, so that they may see My glory which You have given Me, for You loved Me before the foundation of the world."

What does Jesus request of the Father? He wants His people to be with Him—in close fellowship with Him! "Be with me" (Gk. "*meta*") is the same preposition discussed earlier. But this is surely a statement that should cause us to "stop and reflect." *Jesus wants us to be with Him—in close fellowship!* Can we begin to comprehend the magnitude of that statement?

That should, first of all, be a comfort to us when a loved one dies. They are immediately with Christ and in fellowship with Him (2 Cor. 5:8; Phil. 1:23). Moreover, they are precisely where Jesus wants them to be—with Him. One day that will be the privilege and joy of all of us who know Him—we will be in close fellowship with Him and with our loved ones. What a phenomenally wonderful future we have! What a glorious anticipation!

WE WILL WORSHIP HIM

Considerable debate rages today concerning form and style of worship, the type of music; but in that future day there will be unanimity in worship. There will be no argument over choruses or hymns. Believers will worship God majestically in full harmony with Him and one another.

The Old Testament is replete with pictures of worship. As has been previously noted, the millennium is blended with the eternal state. What begins in the millennium will continue in the renovated earth in the eternal state. Jerusalem is pictured as the pinnacle of worship—all highways lead to Jerusalem. Israel's former enemies will repent and acknowledge Jesus Christ as Lord and will come to Jerusalem to worship (Isa. 19:21, 23; 27:13). When God's chosen people, Israel, repent in that future day, He will answer and they will worship the Lord with His blessing resting on them (Isa. 58:1–14).

Gentiles from all the nations will worship the Lord, spreading throughout the world, declaring His glory (Isa. 66:18–19; Zech. 14:16f.). Worship of the Lord will continue for all eternity in the new heaven and the new earth (Isa. 66:22–23).

The worship of God will also have a basis in His blessing. Believers will live amid abundance on the new earth, filled with God's bountiful provision. In that context, believers will "have plenty to eat and be satisfied and praise the name of the Lord your God, who has dealt wondrously with you" (Joel 2:26; Ps. 67:5–7).

The tears that were shed because of suffering on earth will be forgotten. Believers will have a proper perspective on that day, being fully aware that God's plan and purpose is right and good. In that day we will indeed recognize that "God causes all things to work together for good" (Rom. 8:28). The sorrows and tragedies of the old earth will be seen in the glorious light of eternity. Temporal suffering is followed by an eternity of radiant joy that on this finite earth is entirely incomprehensible. But God will be seen as all in all. He will be recognized and worshiped as the holy and righteous and wise God that He is. As we grow in our understanding and knowledge of Him in heaven, our worship will surely increase in magnitude.

WE WILL MARVEL AT HIS GLORY

Shortly after Helen's homegoing, Jeremy and Kim, my son and daughter-in-law, with their children, took me to spend days with them at a condo overlooking the Gulf of Mexico. Several evenings we gazed in wonder at the majestic sunset over the Gulf, the brilliant rays of red and orange filling the sky and coloring the gulf waters. All of the beauty that we saw redounds to the glory of God.

The light of God's glory one day will emanate from Jerusalem but encircle the earth. God will envelop the city with His glory, protecting the city and reminding the Gentile nations that the glory of God comes from Jerusalem (Zech. 2:5). The brilliant blaze of light will be a reminder that God is truth and that His truth originates from Jerusalem. It will be the visible fulfillment of Jesus' statement, "I am the Light of the world" (John 8:12). In heaven no one will any longer walk in darkness. The glory of God will be pervasive, covering the cosmos. At the beginning of the millennium, the glory of God will appear from the east, and the entire earth will be filled with God's glory and will reflect His glory (Ezek. 43:2).

Ezekiel described his vision of the glory of God: "As the appearance of the rainbow in the clouds on a rainy day, so was the appearance of the surrounding radiance. Such was the appearance of the likeness of the glory of the Lord" (Ezek. 1:28). John describes God's glory similarly: "And He who was sitting was like a jasper stone and a sardius in appearance; and there was a rainbow around the throne, like an emerald in appearance" (Rev. 4:3). God's glory is depicted by precious stones like the jasper stone, a translucent rock crystal, or perhaps even a diamond, which may illustrate the majesty and holiness of God.[8] The sardius is a blood-red stone which, note Rogers and Rogers, could depict the wrath and judgment of God. The rainbow "may indicate the halo of emerald which encircled the throne."[9]

Following the millennium, the New Jerusalem is seen coming down from God out of heaven, "having the glory of God. Her brilliance was like a very costly stone, as a stone of crystal-clear jasper" (Rev. 21:11). The brilliance of the city portrays "something in which light is concentrated and thence radiates."[10] God's presence—God's glory—is the embodiment of light, and the New Jerusalem will display that light in a profound brilliance.

Heaven will have no need for artificial light or even the luminaries of the skies. God's glory alone will illuminate the earth, and that will be sufficient (see Rev. 21:23). "God's presence pervades the city and emits constant light in abundance . . . It will be a condition of constant brightness and brilliance," writes Bible commentator Robert Thomas.[11] John the apostle concludes, "And there will no longer be any night; and they will not have need of the light of a lamp nor the light of the sun, because the Lord God will illumine them; and they will reign forever and ever" (Rev. 22:5). The emphasis of this verse is "on the delight this condition will produce for the city's citizens."[12]

In this life people sometimes suffer emotional stress brought on by darkness. Seasonal affective disorder, or SAD, is a known condition that makes its sufferers melancholy, listless, and, yes, sad. An estimated ten million Americans experience it during the shortened days of fall and winter. Some even contemplate suicide. But in that future day there will only be brilliant light, stimulating our emotions for the good, for extreme joy and gladness.

We cannot comprehend the glory of God that will illuminate not only the New Jerusalem but also the entire earth. When we are inside a building in an office, we turn the lights on; in the evening as it begins to get dark, we turn the lights on. In that day, we will enjoy constancy of light and a magnitude of light that we have never beheld before. And it will continue forever. The concluding words "forever and ever" are a reminder that the glory of God will pervade the earth not only during the millennium but also for all eternity.

Earthly eyes that never have seen the majesty of God's glory before will marvel at His glory. We will be enraptured by His glory. In this earthly life we have our emotions stirred from time to time, but when we see the glory of God, we will enjoy unparalleled emotion as we will be overawed by His glory. That will truly be heaven—where it is always better—*in every way!* It is heaven revealed!

CONCLUSION:

How Then Should We LIVE?

Longing is innate in human beings. People who leave their native country by choice or by force have an intense desire to return to their homeland. When, as a result of war, people are relocated, they have a great longing to return to their native land. They feel uncomfortable and out of place in another country. They are foreigners in a strange land, and they long for home.

When a married couple is separated for a period of time, their hearts aches and yearns for the one they love. Helen and I were rarely separated during our forty-five years of marriage; when we were, I found it very difficult. I longed for the day when Helen would return. I would count the days and the hours when we would be together again.

But all of these earthly longings are merely shadows of the real longing. Our earthly longings point to the real, the ultimate longing within us: heaven. Paul expressed it well when he declared, ". . . having the desire to depart and be with Christ, for that is very much better" (Phil. 1:23b). Paul's yearning is expressive. "Desire" stands in the emphatic, prominent position in the Greek text. Paul's heart is drawn to leave this earth and go to heaven to be with Christ. But this is not an occasional emotion that overcomes Paul; it is constant. "Having"[1] means the desire to be with Christ in heaven is constant for Paul. It is his desire continuously.

C. S. Lewis says it well: "Creatures are not born with desires unless satisfaction for those desires exists. . . . If I find in myself a desire which no experience in this world can satisfy, the most probable explanation is that I was made for another world. . . . Probably earthly pleasures were never meant to satisfy it, but only to arouse it, to suggest the real thing."[2]

HEAVENLY CITIZENSHIP

Even though we are living on this earth, Scripture reminds us that "our citizenship is in heaven, from which also we eagerly wait for a Savior, the Lord Jesus Christ" (Phil. 3:20). If we have but an inkling of what awaits us in the glories of heaven, we will be like the apostle Paul who eagerly anticipated that future day of resurrection when believers will be conformed to the "body of His glory" (Phil. 3:21).

Probably our greatest problem is that we are so rooted in this world. It is possible to be so enamored with this life and this world that there is little thought about heaven. Materialism has been destructive to the Christian life, and the very thing that God provided for us to enjoy life has become an end in itself and, in effect, a god.

HEAVENLY THINKING

We are exhorted to "keep seeking the things above, where Christ is, seated at the right hand of God. Set your mind on the things above, not on the things that are on earth" (Col. 3:1b-2). The phrase "things above" means "the heavenly world."[3] It is only as we focus our thoughts on heaven that we will correctly interpret life on earth. It will give us the proper perspective. It will help us avoid the folly of materialism. It will keep us from following the thinking and lifestyle like that of the man who had arranged his funeral and was buried in a Cadillac.

A HEAVENLY CITY, A HEAVENLY COUNTRY

Abraham looked for a city with foundations—one that was permanent (Heb. 11:10). Houses, cities on this earth are temporary. The house that was beautiful when it was built can look dilapidated a few decades later and may be demolished a few decades after that. Nothing is permanent here. But the city that God builds lasts forever. It has a solid foundation that will never crumble or be destroyed. It is permanent; it is eternal. Why should we not want to build our lives and our hopes on that which is permanent?

Abraham and the other patriarchs are acknowledged as heroes of the faith. But how did they come to that? They did not see the promises fulfilled in their lifetime. Yet they looked ahead and "welcomed them from a distance, and having confessed that they were strangers and exiles on the earth. For those who say such things make it clear that they are seeking a country of their own. . . . But as it is, they desire a better country, that is, a heavenly one" (Heb. 11:13b, 14, 16a). These heroes of the faith didn't put their roots down on this earth because they realized they were strangers and exiles on this earth. Instead, they were looking for a better country. And that is our model—we seek a heavenly country. We are to look on ourselves as living in a foreign land; we are not "home" yet. Our home is elsewhere. The patriarchs desired a better country. "Desire" means "to stretch one's self out for, to yearn for."[4] Our danger lies frequently in the other direction. We yearn for a new car, a bigger house, a new computer, more "things." Our challenge is to adopt the biblical injunction to yearn for a heavenly country.

COME!

The ultimate question is of utmost importance: Am I certain I am going to heaven? When my eyelids shut for the last time on this old earth, do I know I will awaken in heaven? The answer rests on whom I am trusting. Jesus Christ alone is the way of salvation that gives us entrance into heaven. He is the one who took our sins upon Himself, paying the price and making atonement for our sins when He died on the cross as our substitute, thereby satisfying the holiness of God. So the key question is: Am I trusting Jesus Christ *alone* for my salvation?

Jesus said, "I am the way, and the truth, and the life; no one comes to the Father but through Me" (John 14:6). The Scripture also says, "For by grace you have been saved through faith; and that not of yourselves, it is the gift of God; not as a result of works, so that no one may boast" (Eph. 2:8–9).

So the invitation is open to anyone and everyone: "The Spirit and the bride say, '*Come*,' And let the one who hears say, '*Come*.' And let the one who is thirsty *come*; let the one who wishes take the water of life without cost" (Rev. 22:17, emphasis added).

If you have never before responded to the invitation of Christ, I urge you to respond. Come. Make your eternal home in heaven a certainty. Enjoy the peace and assurance that your reservation in heaven is complete. Jesus Christ is your Savior and Lord to welcome you into your eternal home!

For those who come and accept the Savior, heaven awaits. Yet it is only as we begin to fathom, in even a small way, the grandeur, the beauty, the joy that awaits us in heaven, that we will learn how to live on this earth. Our life here is brief—like a vapor that vanishes (James 4:14); let's focus on what is eternal. God has opened a fantastic future for us, a future of happiness unparalleled by any earthly measurement. The mind that is focused on the glories that await us in heaven will learn how to live on this earth in this present life. It will anticipate the

wonders, the joy, the love that we will experience forever because it is heaven, where everything is better *in every way. It is heaven revealed!*
 Maranatha!

NOTES

Chapter 1: What Is the Meaning of Heaven?

1. John Koessler, "Come, Lord Jesus—But Not Too Soon," *Christianity Today*, September 2003.

2. Wilbur M. Smith, *The Biblical Doctrine of Heaven* (Chicago: Moody, 1968), 167.

3. Cleon L. Rogers Jr. and Cleon L. Rogers III, *The New Linguistic and Exegetical Key to the Greek New Testament* (Grand Rapids: Zondervan, 1998), 494.

4. Ibid.

5. Joachim Jeremias, "*Paradeisos*," in *Theological Dictionary of the New Testament*, ed. Gerhard Kittel and Gerhard Friedrich, vol. 5 (Grand Rapids: Eerdmans, 1967), 765.

6. Ibid., 767.

7. Ibid., 770.

8. Ibid., 769; Randy Alcorn, *Heaven* (Wheaton, Ill.: Tyndale, 2004), 41–42.

9. Fritz Rienecker and Cleon L. Rogers Jr., *A Linguistic Key to the Greek New Testament* (Grand Rapids: Zondervan, 1980), 467.

10. Ibid., 860.

11. Leon Morris, *The Revelation of St. John* (Grand Rapids: Eerdmans, 1969), 249.

12. Erwin W. Lutzer, *One Minute After You Die* (Chicago: Moody, 1997), 83. Randy Alcorn calculates the city as a 1,400 mile cube, and allowing a 12-foot story, the city would have over 600,000 stories, and "billions of people could occupy the New Jerusalem, with many square miles per person" (Alcorn, *Heaven* [Wheaton, Ill.: Tyndale, 2004], 242).

13. Lutzer, *One Minute After You Die*, 83.

14. Robert L. Thomas, *Revelation 8–22: An Exegetical Commentary*, vol 2. (Chicago: Moody, 1995), 468.

15. Ibid., 462.

16. Ibid., 469.

17. F. Wilbur Gingrich and Frederick W. Danker, *A Greek-English Lexicon of the New Testament and Other Early Christian Literature*, 2nd ed. (Chicago: Univ. of Chicago, 1979), 636–37.

18. Gottlob Schrenk, "*patrias*," in *Theological Dictionary of the New Testament*, ed. Gerhard Kittel and Gerhard Friedrich, vol. 5 (Grand Rapids: Eerdmans, 1967), 1017.

Chapter 2: What Is the Transition to Heaven?

1. Cleon L. Rogers Jr. and Cleon L. Rogers III, *The New Linguistic and Exegetical Key to the Greek New Testament* (Grand Rapids: Zondervan, 1998), 520.

2. Paul N. Benware, *Understanding End Times Prophecy* (Chicago: Moody, 2006), 347.

3. F. Wilbur Gingrich and Frederick W. Danker, *A Greek-English Lexicon of the New Testament and Other Early Christian Literature*, 2nd ed. (Chicago: Univ. of Chicago, 1979), 638.

4. The Greek particles *men . . . de* reflect this contrast.

5. Rogers and Rogers, *The New Linguistic and Exegetical Key*, 389.

6. Heinrich Schlier, "*kerdos*," in *Theological Dictionary of the New Testament*, ed. Gerhard Kittel and Gerhard Friedrich, vol. 5 (Grand Rapids: Eerdmans, 1967), 672–73.

7. Gerald F. Hawthorne, "Philippians" in *Word Biblical Commentary* (Waco, Tex.: Word, 1983), 46.

8. Erwin W. Lutzer, *One Minute After You Die* (Chicago: Moody, 1997), 45.

9. Gingrich and Danker, *A Greek-English Lexicon*, 559.

10. Otto Michel, "*oikos*," in *Theological Dictionary of the New Testament*, ed. Gerhard Kittel and Gerhard Friedrich, vol. 5 (Grand Rapids: Eerdmans, 1967), 146.

11. Ibid., 547.

12. Gingrich and Danker, *A Greek-English Lexicon*, 276.

13. Michaelis, "*exodus*," in *Theological Dictionary of the New Testament*, ed., Kittel and Friedrich, vol. 5 (Grand Rapids: Eerdmans, 1967), 105.

14. Rogers and Rogers, *The New Linguistic and Exegetical Key*, 151.

15. Ibid., 595.

16. J. Oswald Sanders, *Heaven: Better by Far* (Grand Rapids: Discovery House, 1993), 44.

17. Gingrich and Danker, *A Greek-English Lexicon*, 508.

18. Rogers and Rogers, *The New Linguistic and Exegetical Key*, 65.

19. William R. Moody, *The Life of D. L. Moody* (New York: Revell, 1900), 552–53; as quoted in Lyle W. Dorsett, *A Passion for Souls* (Chicago: Moody, 1997), 380–81.

20. Rogers and Rogers, *The New Linguistic and Exegetical Key*, 445.

21. Ibid.

22. Leon Morris, *The Gospel According to John* (Grand Rapids: Eerdmans, 1971), 736.

23. Robert J. Morgan, *Then Sings My Soul*, book 2 (Nashville: Nelson, 2004), 175.

24. D. Edmond Hiebert, *Second Timothy* (Chicago: Moody, 1958), 123.

25. Lutzer, *One Minute After You Die*, 44.

26. Rogers and Rogers, *The New Linguistic and Exegetical Key*, 507.

Chapter 3: Where Is Heaven?

1. C. F. Keil and F. Delitzsch, *Biblical Commentary on the Old Testament: The Books of the Kings* (Grand Rapids: Eerdmans, 1970), 326.

2. John Peter Lange, *Commentary on the Holy Scriptures: The Books of the Kings*, vol. 2 (1845; repr. Grand Rapids: Zondervan, 1960), 68.

3. Franz Delitzsch, *Biblical Commentary on the Prophecies of Isaiah*, vol. 1 (1877; repr. Grand Rapids: Eerdmans, 1969), 189.

4. Lamar Eugene Cooper Sr., *Ezekiel: The New American Commentary* (Nashville: Broadman and Holman, 1994), 60.

5. Leon Wood, *A Commentary on Daniel* (Grand Rapids: Zondervan, 1973), 193.

6. *Katabainonta* ("saw") is a present active participle, picturing the continuing descent of the angel.

7. The perfect participle "indicates the completed state ('to be opened')"; cf. Cleon L. Rogers Jr. and Cleon L. Rogers III, *The New Linguistic and Exegetical Key to the Greek New Testament* (Grand Rapids: Zondervan, 1998), 180.

8. Martin Luther as quoted in R. C. H. Lenski, *The Interpretation of St. Matthew's Gospel* (Minneapolis: Augsburg, 1943), 130.

9. W. D. Davies and Dale C. Allison, *A Critical and Exegetical Commentary on the Gospel of Matthew*, vol. 1 (Edinburgh: T&T Clark, 1988), 329.

10. Lenski, *St. Matthew's Gospel*, 133.

11. D. Edmond Hiebert, *Mark: A Portrait of the Servant* (Chicago: Moody, 1974), 37.

Chapter 4: What Is the Kingdom Christ Promised?

1. Hermann Cremer, *Biblico-Theological Lexicon of New Testament Greek* (New York: Charles Scribner's Sons, 1895), 132.

2. The name David may be a title of Messiah and therefore a reference to Christ since Christ is of the lineage of David and He will rule as king.

3. F. Wilbur Gingrich and Frederick W. Danker, *A Greek-English Lexicon of the New Testament and Other Early Christian Literature* , 2nd ed. (Chicago: Univ. of Chicago, 1979), 699. The word "gentle" (Gk. *praus*) pictures a tamed animal that is now under control.

4. Cleon L. Rogers Jr. and Cleon L. Rogers III, *The New Linguistic and Exegetical Key to the Greek New Testament* (Grand Rapids: Zondervan, 1998), 19.

5. Merrill F. Unger, *Zechariah* (Grand Rapids: Zondervan, 1963), 165.

6. Charles L. Feinberg, *The Minor Prophets* (Chicago: Moody, 1976), 123.

7. Rogers and Rogers, *New Linguistic Key*, 181.

8. Gingrich and Danker, *A Greek-English Lexicon*, 883–84.

Chapter 5: What Kind of Body Will We Have?

1. Lewis Sperry Chafer, "Populating the Third Heaven," *Bibliotheca Sacra*, 1951, no. 108:147.

2. B. F. Westcott, as cited in Cleon L. Rogers Jr. and Cleon L. Rogers III, *The New Linguistic and Exegetical Key to the Greek New Testament*, 2nd ed. (Grand Rapids: Zondervan, 1998), 595.

3. F. Wilbur Gingrich and Frederick W. Danker, *A Greek-English Lexicon of the New Testament and Other Early Christian Literature* (Chicago: Univ. of Chicago, 1979), 39.

4. Max Zerwick, *Greek Grammar of the N.T.*, 3rd rev. ed. (1966; repr. Roma: Editrice Pontificio Instituto Biblico, 1988), 530.

5. Rogers and Rogers, *The New Linguistic Key and Exegetical Key to the Greek N.T.* (Grand Rapids: Zondervan, 1998), 388.

6. Ibid., p. 456.

7. Charles Hodge, *First Corinthians* (London: Banner of Truth Trust, 1958), 347.

8. Frederick L. Godet, *Commentary on the First Epistle of St. Paul to the Corinthians*, vol. 2 (Grand Rapids: Zondervan, 1957), 412.

9. Robert G. Gromacki, *Called To Be Saints* (Grand Rapids: Baker, 1977), 194.

10. Hodge, *First Corinthians*, 347.

11. Archibald Robertson and Alfred Plummer, *A Critical and Exegetical Commentary on the First Epistle of St. Paul to the Corinthians* (Edinburgh: T & T Clark, 1967), 372.

12. Ibid.

Chapter 6: What Is the Relationship of the Millennium to Heaven?

1. Herbert M. Wolf, *Interpreting Isaiah* (Grand Rapids: Zondervan, 1985), 251.

2. Ibid., 300.

3. Erwin W. Lutzer, *One Minute After You Die* (Chicago: Moody, 1997), 89.

4. Herman A. Hoyt, *The End Times* (Winona Lake, Ind.: BMH, 1987), 230.

5. Erich Sauer, *The Triumph of the Crucified* (1961; repr. Exeter: Paternoster Press, 1964), 178.

6. Merrill F. Unger, *Unger's Commentary on the Old Testament* (Chattanooga: AMG, 2002), 1334.

Chapter 7: What and When Are the New Heaven and the New Earth?

1. While some aspects of Isaiah's statements are decidedly millennial, as when he depicts an infant, an old man, and a youth dying, other aspects of Isaiah's statement should be seen as combining both millennial and eternal perspectives. John's mention of the new heaven and the new earth *after* the millennium demands this.

2. Paul N. Benware, *Understanding End Times Prophecy* (Chicago: Moody, 2006), 340.

3. Kenneth S. Wuest, *Prophetic Light in the Present Darkness* (Grand Rapids: Eerdmans, 1955), 155.

4. Anthony A. Hoekema, *The Bible and the Future* (Grand Rapids: Eerdmans, 1979), 280.

5. Erich Sauer, *The King of the Earth* (1961; repr. Exeter: Paternoster Press, 1964). Sauer capably develops this thesis throughout his book.

6. Wayne Grudem, *Systematic Theology* (Grand Rapids: Zondervan, 1994), 1160.

7. Erich Sauer, *The Triumph of the Crucified* (1961; repr. Exeter: Paternoster Press, 1964), 179.

8. Henry C. Thiessen, *Lectures In Systematic Theology* (Grand Rapids: Eerdmans, 1949), 516.

9. J. A. Seiss, *Lectures on the Apocalypse,* vol. 3 (Philadelphia: Philadelphia School of the Bible, 1865), 371.

10. *Allagesontai* from *allasso.* See F. Wilbur Gingrich and Frederick W. Danker, *A Greek-English Lexicon of the New Testament and Other Early Christian Literature* 2nd ed. (Chicago: Univ. of Chicago, 1979), 39.

11. Grudem, *Systematic Theology,* 1161.

12. Louis T. Talbot, *God's Plan of the Ages* (Grand Rapids: Eerdmans, 1936), 196.

13. David Jeremiah, *Escape the Coming Night* (Nashville: W Publishing, 1997), 243.

14. Alan F. Johnson and Robert E. Webber, *What Christians Believe* (Grand Rapids: Zondervan, 1993), 421.

15. Cleon L. Rogers, Jr. and Cleon L. Rogers III, *The New Linguistic and Exegetical Key to the Greek New Testament* (Grand Rapids: Zondervan, 1998), 366.

16. Randy Alcorn, *Heaven* (Wheaton, Ill.: Tyndale, 2004), 137.

17. Herbert Preisker, "*klepto, kleptes,*" *Theological Dictionary of the New Testament,* ed., Gerhard Kittel, vol. 3 (Grand Rapids: Eerdmans, 1965), 755–56.

18. Franz Deliitzsch, *Biblical Commentary on the Prophecies of Isaiah 2*, vol. 1 (Grand Rapids: Eerdmans, 1969), 426.

19. Herbert Wolf, *Interpreting Isaiah* (Grand Rapids: Zondervan, 1985), 301.

20. Merrill F. Unger, *Zechariah: Prophet of Messiah's Glory* (Grand Rapids: Zondervan, 1963), 251–52.

21. C. F. Keil, *The Twelve Minor Prophets*, vol. 2 (Grand Rapids: Eerdmans, repr. 1969), 154.

22. C. Von Orelli, *The Twelve Minor Prophets* (Minneapolis: Klock & Klock, 1977), 276.

23. Mitchell Dahood, *Psalms I*, The Anchor Bible Series (Garden City, N.Y.: Doubleday, 1966), 281.

24. Tim LaHaye, *Revelation Unveiled* (Grand Rapids: Zondervan, 1999), 356–57.

25. Randy Alcorn, *Heaven* (Wheaton, Ill.: Tyndale, 2004), 138.

26. Erich Sauer, *The King of the Earth* (1961; repr. Exeter: Paternoster Press, 1964), 152.

Chapter 8: What Will Heaven and the New Earth Look Like?

1. Robert L. Thomas, *Revelation 8-22: An Exegetical Commentary*, vol. 2 (Chicago: Moody, 1995), 475.

2. Erwin W. Lutzer, *One Minute After You Die* (Chicago: Moody, 1997), 44.

3. Merrill F. Unger, *Zechariah: Prophet of Messiah's Glory* (Grand Rapids: Zondervan, 1963), 256.

4. Ibid., 255.

5. John F. Walvoord, *The Revelation of Jesus Christ* (Chicago: Moody, 1966), 329.

6. Charles C. Ryrie, *Revelation* (Chicago: Moody, 1996), 142.

7. Franz Delitzsch, *Biblical Commentary on the Prophecies of Isaiah*, vol. 2 (Grand Rapids: Eerdmans, 1969 repr.), 78.

8. W. E. Vine, *Isaiah: Prophecies, Promises, Warnings* (London: Oliphants, 1946), 85.

Chapter 9: What Will Life Be Like in Heaven?

1. The verb "functions as a divine passive"; Cleon L. Rogers Jr. and Cleon L. Rogers III, *The New Linguistic and Exegetical Key to the Greek New Testament* (Grand Rapids: Zondervan, 1998), 121.

2. Charles L. Feinberg, *The Minor Prophets* (Chicago: Moody, 1976), 288.

3. Rogers and Rogers, *The New Linguistic Key*, 48.

4. Francis Brown, S. R. Driver, and Charles A. Briggs, *A Hebrew and English Lexicon of the Old Testament* (Oxford: Clarendon, 1968), 562.

5. F. Wilbur Gingrich and Frederick W. Danker, *A Greek-English Lexicon of the New Testament and Other Early Christian Literature*, 2nd ed. (Chicago: Univ. of Chicago, 1979), 883–84.

6. Herbert M. Wolf, *Interpreting Isaiah* (Grand Rapids: Zondervan, 1985), 251.

7. Rogers and Rogers, *The New Linguistic and Exegetical Key*, 501.

8. Randy Alcorn, *Heaven* (Wheaton, Ill.: Tyndale, 2004), 274.

9. Augustine, *City of God*, 22:19, 2; 22:20, 3.

10. Alister McGrath, *A Brief History of Heaven*, (New York: Wiley-Blackwell, 2003), 37–38.

11. Thomas Aquinas, *Summa Theologica*, supplement, q.81, art. 1.

12. Hank Hanegraaff, *Resurrection* (Nashville: Thomas Nelson, 2002), 133–34.

13. Alcorn, *Heaven*, 290.

Chapter 10: What Is the Continuity Between This Life and Life in Heaven?

1. William Robertson Nicoll, quoted in Oswald Sanders, *Heaven* (Grand Rapids: Discovery House, 1993), 36.

2. Sanders. *Heaven*, 36.

3. Erwin Lutzer, *One Minute After You Die* (Chicago: Moody, 1997), 63.

4. Ibid.

5. As James Montgomery Boice wrote in *Foundations of the Christian Faith*, "We *will* know each other. Bill will know Sally. Sally will know Bill. We will know parents and children, friends and relatives, and those who have died in the Lord before us." Boice, *Foundations* (Downers Grove, Ill.: InterVarsity, 1986), 716 .

6. Cleon L. Rogers Jr. and Cleon L. Rogers III, *The New Linguistic and Exegetical Key to the Greek New Testament* (Grand Rapids: Zondervan, 1998), 380.

7. Randy Alcorn, *Heaven* (Wheaton, Ill.: Tyndale, 2004), 337.

8. John MacArthur, *The Glory of Heaven* (Wheaton, Ill.: Crossway, 1996), 140.

9. Lutzer, *One Minute After You Die*, 64.

10. Rogers and Rogers, *The New Linguistic and Exegetical Key*, 651.

11. Wilbur Smith, *The Biblical Doctrine of Heaven* (Chicago: Moody, 1968), 192.

12. Ibid., 195.

13. Lutzer, *One Minute After You Die*, 67.

14. Alcorn, *Heaven*, 396–97.

Chapter 11: What Will We Do in Heaven?

1. Paul N. Benware, *Understanding End Times Prophecy* (Chicago: Moody, 2006), 340.

2. Randy Alcorn, *Heaven* (Wheaton, Ill.: Tyndale, 2004), 189.

3. Ibid., 188–89.

4. Fritz Rienecker and Cleon L. Rogers Jr., *A Linguistic Key to the Greek New Testament* (Grand Rapids: Zondervan, 1980), 862.

5. F. Wilbur Gingrich and Fredrick W. Danker, *A Greek-English Lexicon of the New Testament and Other Early Christian Literature*, 2nd ed. (Chicago: Univ. of Chicago, 1979), 508.

6. Alcorn, *Heaven*, 234–35.

7. H. Strathmann, "*Latreuo, Latreia*," *The Theological Dictionary of the New Testament*, ed. Gerhard Kittel and Gerhard Friedrich, trans. Geoffrey W. Bromiley, vol. 4. (Grand Rapids: Eerdmans, 1967), 63.

8. Ibid.

9. Herbert M. Wolf, *Interpreting Isaiah* (Grand Rapids: Zondervan, 1985), 251.

10. Alcorn, *Heaven*, 400.

Chapter 12: What Will Our Relationships with Others Be Like?

1. Bruce Milne, *The Message of Heaven and Hell* (Downers Grove, Ill: InterVarsity, 2002), 195.

2. Winifred Forceythe, as quoted in Alister E. McGrath, *A Brief History of Heaven* (Malden, Mass.: Blackwell, 2003), 152.

3. The present imperative "*chairete*" reflects these words. Cleon L. Rogers Jr. and Cleon L. Rogers III, *The New Linguistic Key to the Greek New Testament*, 65; Max Zerwick, *A Grammatical Analysis of the Greek New Testament* (Roma: Editrice Pontificio Istituto Biblico, 1988), 98.

4. Hans Conzelmann, *Theological Dictionary of the New Testament*, vol. 9, ed. Gerhard Friedrich (Grand Rapids: Eerdmans, 1974), 366.

5. Rogers and Rogers, *The New Linguistic and Exegetical Key*, 65; F. Wilbur Gingrich and Frederick W. Danker, *A Greek-English Lexicon of the New Testament*, rev. ed. (Chicago: Univ. of Chicago, 1979), 448. The latter suggests it may mean "to take hold of, grasp, seize forcibly."

6. J. Oswald Sanders, *Heaven* (Grand Rapids: Discovery House, 1993), 36.

7. Erwin W. Lutzer, *One Minute After You Die* (Chicago: Moody, 1997), 64.

8. James Montgomery Boice, *Foundations of the Christian Faith* (Downers Grove, Ill.: InterVarsity, 1986), 719.

9. Charles C. Ryrie, *Ryrie Study Bible* (Chicago: Moody, 1995), 1082.

10. John H. Gerstner, *Heaven and Hell: Jonathan Edwards on the Afterlife* (Grand Rapids: Baker, 1991), 13.

11. John F. MacArthur, *The Glory of Heaven* (Wheaton, Ill.: Crossway, 1996), 138.

12. Randy Alcorn, *Heaven* (Wheaton, Ill.: Tyndale, 2004), 331.

13. John F. Walvoord, *The Nations in Prophecy* (Grand Rapids: Zondervan, 1967), 169–70.

14. Gordon R. Lewis and Bruce A. Demarest, *Integrative Theology*, vol. 3 (Grand Rapids: Zondervan, 1994), 482.

15. John MacArthur, *The Glory of Heaven* (Wheaton, Ill.: Crossway, 1996), 138.

Chapter 13: What Will Our Relationship with God Be Like?

1. Cleon L. Rogers Jr. and Cleon L. Rogers III, *The New Linguistic and Exegetical Key to the Greek New Testament* (Grand Rapids: Zondervan, 1998), 9.

2. B. F. Westcott, *The Epistles of St. John* (Grand Rapids: Eerdmans, 1966), 99.

3. Robert L. Thomas, *Revelation 8–22: An Exegetical Commentary*, vol. 2 (Chicago: Moody, 1995), 487.

4. Rogers and Rogers, *The New Linguistic and Exegetical Key*, 790.

5. J. Schneider, "*Homoios*," in *Theological Dictionary of the New Testament*, ed. Gerhard Kittel and Gerhard Friedrich, vol. 5 (Grand Rapids: Eerdmans, 1967), 188.

6. Rogers and Rogers, *The New Linguistic and Exegetical Key*, 859.

7. F. Wilbur Gingrich and Frederick W. Danker, *A Greek-English Lexicon of the New Testament*, 2nd ed. (Chicago: Univ. of Chicago, 1979), 508.

8. Rogers and Rogers, *The New Linguistic and Exegetical Key*, 822.

9. Ibid., 822–23.

10. Ibid., 860.

11. Thomas, *Revelation*, 475.

12. Ibid., 488.

Conclusion: How Then Should We Live?

1. The verb "*echon*" is a present active participle, denoting the kind of action. It is constant.

2. C. S. Lewis, *Mere Christianity* (New York: Touchstone, 1980), 121.

3. Cleon L. Rogers Jr. and Cleon L. Rogers III, *The New Linguistic and Exegetical Key to the Greek New Testament* (Grand Rapids: Zondervan, 1998), 577.

4. Ibid., 709.

SELECTED BIBLIOGRAPHY

Alcorn, Randy. *Heaven*. Wheaton, Ill.: Tyndale, 2004.

_____. *50 Days of Heaven*. Wheaton, Ill.: Tyndale, 2006.

Boles, Kenny. *Heaven: What A Wonderful Place!* Joplin, Mo.: College Press, 1999.

Bounds, E. M. *A Place Called Heaven*. New Kensington, PA: Whitaker, 2003.

Buchanan, Mark. *Things Unseen*. Sisters, Ore: Multnomah, 2002.

Connelly, Douglas. *Heaven*. Downers Grove, Ill.: InterVarsity, 2000.

Conyers, A. J. *The Eclipse Of Heaven*. Downers Grove, Ill.: InterVarsity, 1992.

Edwards, Jonathan. *Heaven: A World Of Love*. Amityville, N.Y.: Calvary, 1999.

Gerstner, John. *Heaven and Hell: Jonathan Edwards on the Afterlife*. Grand Rapids: Baker, 1980.

Ice, Thomas and Timothy J. Demy. *Heaven & Eternity.* Rev. ed. Grand Rapids: Kregel, 2000.

Jeremiah, David. *Escape The Coming Night.* Nashville: W Publishing, 1997.

Kelsey, Morton. *What Is Heaven Like?* Hyde Park, NY: New City Press, 1997.

Kreeft, Peter. *Everything You Ever Wanted To Know About Heaven.* San Francisco: Ignatius, 1990.

Lutzer, Erwin W. *One Minute After You Die.* Chicago: Moody, 1997.

_____. *Your Eternal Reward.* Chicago: Moody, 1998.

MacArthur, John. *The Glory of Heaven.* Wheaton, Ill.: Crossway, 1996.

McGrath, Alister E. *A Brief History Of Heaven.* Malden, Mass.: Blackwell, 2003.

Moody, D. L. *Heaven.* Rev. ed. Chicago: Moody, 1995.

Morrow, Barry. *Heaven Observed.* Colorado Springs: NavPress, 2001.

Ryle, J. C., et al. *Shall We Know One Another In Heaven?* Greenville, N.C.: Ambassador, 1996.

Sanders, J. *Heaven: Better By Far.* Grand Rapids: Discovery House, 1993.

Smith, Wilbur M. *The Biblical Doctrine of Heaven.* Chicago: Moody, 1968.

Stowell, Joseph M. *Eternity.* Chicago: Moody, 1995.

Tada, Joni Eareckson. *Heaven.* Grand Rapids: Zondervan, 1995.

ONE MINUTE AFTER YOU DIE

AND ONE MINUTE AFTER YOU DIE STUDY GUIDE AND DVD

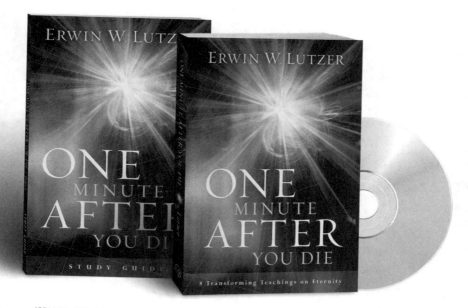

ISBN-13: 978-0-8024-6308-1   ISBN-13: 978-0-8024-6305-0   ISBN-13:978-0-8024-6309-8

Someone you know is about to pass away. Will they enter delight? Or horror? Many people spend more time planning for a vacation than preparing for eternity. Perhaps it doesn't seem real that we will still exist—fully conscious and alive—beyond the grave. But it's true, and it calls for careful consideration. In this updated edition of *One Minute After You Die*, bestselling author Erwin Lutzer urges readers to study what the Bible says on this critical subject.

MOODY
PUBLISHERS

MoodyPublishers.com

THE MOODY HANDBOOK
OF THEOLOGY

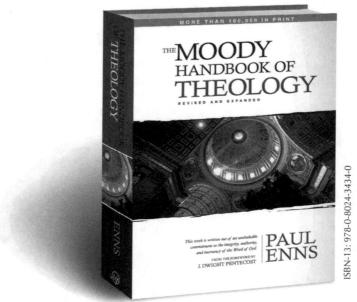

ISBN-13: 978-0-8024-3434-0

The Moody Handbook of Theology leads the reader into the appreciation and understanding of the essentials of Christian theology. It introduces the reader to the five dimensions that provide a comprehensive view of theology: biblical theology, systematic theology, historical theology, dogmatic theology, and contemporary theology. Paul Enns provides a concise doctrinal reference tool for newcomer and scholar. The book includes new material on the openness of God, health and wealth theology, the emergent church, various rapture interpretations, feminism, and more.

MOODY
PUBLISHERS

MoodyPublishers.com